The
Reduced History of
FOOTBALL

First published in 2004
Second edition 2011

Prion Books
An imprint of the
Carlton Publishing Group
20 Mortimer Street
London W1T 3JW

A CIP catalogue record for this book
is available from the British Library

ISBN 978-1-85375-826-3

Printed in China

Words: Justyn Barnes & Aubrey Day
Illustrations: Tony Husband
Designer: James Pople
Production: Janette Burgin
Commisioning Editor: Martin Corteel

Monopoly © 2004. Hasbro all rights
reserved. Many thanks to Hasbro for kind
permission to use their monopoly board
(see page 91).

The
Reduced History of
FOOTBALL

The story of the world's greatest game freshly squeezed into 120 minutes

Justyn Barnes & Aubrey Day Illustrations by Tony Husband

PRION

This book is dedicated to everyone who seeks the meaning of life, football and Katie Price's career…

INTRODUCTION

Football, eh? Marvellous. It's also very, very old. Even older than Sir Bobby Charlton. By our reckoning, some 900 years old (okay, so maybe just about the same age as the great Sir Bob).

And what a fun-packed, net-busting, head-scratching, team-bonding, headline-launching, nation-dividing, dubious-decision-making, trophy-laden, filthy-rotten-lucre-spending, owl-killing 900 years it's been. How could we possibly cram it all into one book – especially a book as beautifully formed but, let's face it, as small as this one?

Well, fortunately dear reader, that was our problem not yours. We sifted through the parchments and papers (and Googled stuff) so you don't have to. Instead, sit back, relax and enjoy the abbreviated (very abbreviated, actually...) highlights of the world's greatest sport freshly squeezed into 90 minutes (plus extra time).

Um... goal!

KICK OFF

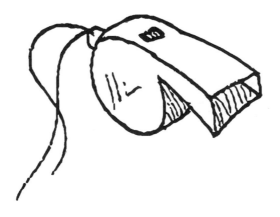

Pancakes for goalposts!
Ye olde pancake-tossers invent footballe

Football, or ye olde footballe as it was almost certainly known in the olden days, was first played in England in the 1100s as part of Shrovetide festivities. Ye olde footballe was a free-for-all. Often hundreds of pancake-tossing villagers or townspeople would play and they made the rules up as they went along. The object of the game might be to carry a ball from one end of the village or town to the other, but how you got there was up to you. Rather than trying to deliver Beckham-esque 40-yard passes to a team-mate standing next to the slaughterhouse, most of the kicking was aimed at the backside of the person mad enough to take possession of the ball. It was like a mixture of hurling, American Football and crown green bowling. Only more violent.

Royal spoilsports ban football

At times in the Middle Ages, football was banned in England, Scotland and France by royal decree! Forsooth, check out this, er, never-before-seen, but clearly authentic legal text...

I hereby decree that out of reverence and honour for God and the blessed Mary, eternal virgin, and for the health of ourselves and our ancestors and heirs, that the liberty of playing the game of ye olde footballe shall heretoforth be prohibited upon England's green pastures. I hereby grant to all bishops full power to constrain the aforesaid sport which encourages my subjects to violent acts... and interferes with archery practice. For this reason I desire and firmly command that it shall be legal for the bishops and their successors to enter the homes of men who possess ye studded boots and to take seizin of any footballes found pertaining to this dangerous activity. So there.

By order of the King

Play footie, be happy

Football starts to catch on in public schools...

IT'S OFFICIAL - FOOTBALL'S EDUCATIONAL! OR SO RICHARD MULCASTER, THE HEADMASTER OF ST PAUL'S SCHOOL IN LONDON, BELIEVED IN THE SIXTEENTH CENTURY. THE TEACHERS ALL THOUGHT HE WAS QUITE MAD - 'MAD MULCASTER' THEY CALLED HIM (ER, PROBABLY). MAD MUL WROTE A TREATISE, WHICH IS LIKE A PAMPHLET BUT BIGGER, CLAIMING THAT FOOTBALL PROVIDED NOT ONLY POSITIVE EDUCATIONAL VALUES BUT ALSO THAT IT COULD BE USED TO PROMOTE HEALTH AND STRENGTH. THE REACTION? WELL, NATURALLY EVERYONE THOUGHT HE WAS QUITE MAD, BUT SOON THE PUPILS GREW HEALTHIER AND STRONGER FROM PLAYING FOOTBALL, AND OTHER HEAD-MASTERS AT OTHER POSH ENGLISH SCHOOLS STARTED TO ENCOURAGE THEIR TOFFEE-NOSED PUPILS TO $\rightarrow$

→ PLAY FOOTBALL TOO. NO PROPER RULES HAD BEEN INVENTED BACK THEN SO, AT FIRST, THE SNOOTY BOYS KICKED THE BALL, PICKED IT UP, THREW IT, SAT ON IT AND USED IT AS A HANGING BASKET OUTSIDE THE BOARDING HOUSE WHEN IT GOT PUNCTURED. BUT OVER THE NEXT FEW CENTURIES, THE GAME WAS TAKEN UP BY MORE AND MORE ENGLISH PUBLIC SCHOOLS AND RULES AND REGULATIONS WERE STANDARDIZED.
GOD BLESS YOU MR MULCASTER! YOU MAD OLD BEAN...

"Let's play 11 v 11... HOORAH!"

By 1841, football was legal again and those dandies at Eton introduced the 11-a-side game. The pupils thought it was divine

Dearest Aunt Mabel,

Returned to Eton for the autumn term and we've started playing a super new game. This afternoon, I dashed off to the gymnasium for PE. Master Glossop is normally such a stick in the mud, and we were all rather dreading another 35-lap race round the Quad. Instead, he produced a football and we all popped off to the playing fields. My chum Topper piped up, "What ho, old man. Why don't we divide into two teams of 11." Old Glossop thought it was a frightfully good idea, but there were 23 of us. Luckily, Fatty Briggs had indigestion after eating eight cream scones at luncheon, so he just sat and watched. I say, Aunt Mabel, it was awfully good fun, kicking the ball as hard as we could and crashing into each other. I was quite the ruffian! And poor old Wilberforce Wattle had to be carted off to matron's to get his head stitched after an unfortunate collision with Bingo's elbow.

Anyway, must dash – Topper's invited Bingo and I to his dorm to bob for apples.

Love to Uncle Horatio.

Pip pip,

Bertie

Cambridge rules OK!

After years of anarchic pig's bladder-pummelling, men from public and non-public schools met to create the "Cambridge Rules" which formed the basis for future rulifications...

MEETING TO CODIFY LAWS OF FOOTBALL

Trinity College, Cambridge
13 June 1848

Chairman: WR – Prof. W.Rooney, Headmaster, Winchester
Delegates: SG – Prof. S.Gerrard, Head Of Human Sciences, Eton; Sir JW – Sir J.Wilkinson, Knight of the Realm and Master Of Physics, Rugby; MO – Prof. M.Owen, Master Of Mathematics, Harrow; DB – Prof. D.Beckham, Master of English Language, Leytonstone Grammar School

MINUTES
RESTARTING PLAY
WR: Raises the first topic of restarting the game when the ball goes out of play – that is beyond the area bounded only by four corner flags.
SG: Suggests a straight throw-in by hand should be taken.
DB: Agrees SG's proposal has merit, but says he has found restarting play by kicking the stationary ball after it goes out of play to be effective.
Sir JW: Has also found kicking most effective.
MO: Favours the straight throw-in.
WR: Feels DB's proposal is too radical at this time and cast his vote for the straight throw-in.

TACKLING OPPONENT
SG: Proposes that players should continue to be allowed to take the ball from an opponent by any means. Advocates holding, pushing, tripping because it's spiffing good fun.
Sir JW: Agrees it is spiffing good fun.
MO, WR, DB: All strongly disagree and WR declares that such practices be prohibited.

CATCHING THE BALL
WR: Proposes that players be allowed their hands only to catch a kick but not run with it.
MO: Suggests WR is a big girl's blouse.

1

The tale of the tape

In 1865, the Football Association was formed and wooden crossbars were soon erected to celebrate...

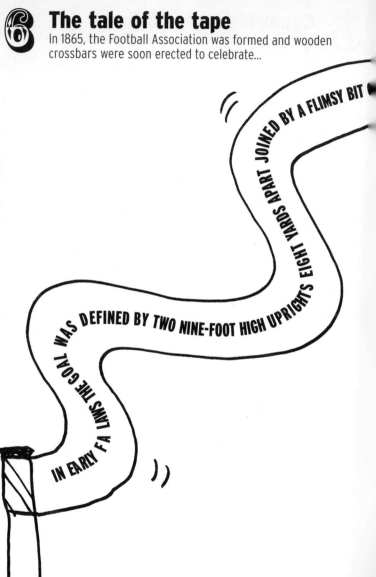

IN EARLY FA LAWS THE GOAL WAS DEFINED BY TWO NINE-FOOT HIGH UPRIGHTS EIGHT YARDS APART JOINED BY A FLIMSY BIT

APE. SOON A STURDIER WOODEN CROSSBAR WAS INTRODUCED.

Tricky vicar is first FA cup hero

On 16 March 1872, "The Prince Of Dribblers" Reverend R.W.S Vidal inspires Wanderers FC to a 1-0 win over Royal Engineers in the first-ever FA Cup final. This is a (very) exclusive extract from Vicar Vidal's very next sermon. Verily.

"Verily we were blessed with a bye to the semi-finals of the Football Association Challenge Cup whereupon our foes were Queens Park of Glasgow. Twas a battle to test the noblest of hearts but we won by nil goals to nil for the infidels couldst not afford to stay in London for a replay. Blessed are the meek indeed. Forsooth, in the final match at Kennington Oval before a 2000-strong congregation, we didst face the Royal Engineers. We met their fiery torches of damnation with the sturdy steed of our faith in almighty God (and the finest players to have graduated from England's public schools and universities). This time, a nil-nil win would not be enough. So it came to pass, that I, the 'Prince Of Dribblers', prayed to the Prince Of Peace and he didst say unto me 'Man On'. And thus it came to pass that I didst pass the ball to my brethren M.P. Betts who scored the winner, whereupon I felt the holy spirit leap inside me and I didst cry, 'Geeetttt in theeerre!' Amen."

Hurts like Corinthian spirit!

Early hero Hon A.F. Kinnaird knocks 'em dead!

A century before that charming Vinnie Jones showed what can be achieved by lack of talent and brutality (and that's just his acting – arf!), the robust style of the Hon A.F. Kinnaird, later an Earl and President of the FA, made him a hero of the amateur game. He was known as "the W.G. Grace of footie" although unlike Grace his facial hair was a vivid red that you could make out from space. Kinnaird played in nine FA Cup finals and earned five winners medals (which not even Vinnie managed).

In those days, hacking was legal, and Kinnaird could be a pretty intimidating opponent. Legend has it that when a player from another team called on Kinnaird's mum she confessed she lived in fear that her son would one day come back from "that horrid rough game" with a broken leg. To which the opposition player legendarily replied: "Don't worry Ma'am, it won't be his own."

That's the (Corinthian) spirit!

Let there be light!
Sheffield hosts the first floodlit match

Some 20,000 spectators were witness to the first "floodlit" game on a cold October night in Sheffield on 14 October 1878. History was made as a match between two local sides at Bramall Lane was played under electric lights. Four big lamps with considerably bigger bulbs than you have in your house were mounted on 30-foot wooden towers and erected in each corner of the ground and powered by electric generators. The fans loved the, ahem, bright idea and subsequent experiments at other grounds were also greeted with enthusiasm by night owls. The first such experiment in London however proved there was still some work to be done as a combination of uneven lighting and high winds illustrated that the system wasn't yet foolproof. Most illuminating... (sorry).

10 Artisans take t'coop oop north

Blackburn Olympic tradesmen hammer their Old Etonian aristocratic rivals in't 1883 FA Coop final

Eleven years of Southern dominance was ended by the plumbers and weavers of Blackburn Olympic, who plumbed and weaved away to become the first team ever to take FA Cup oop north. Top-hatted Old Etonian supporters in the enclosure at Kennington Oval spilt champers and canapés in disbelief as the 1882 winners were beaten 2–1 after extra time. Not even our old pal, Hon. A.F. Kinnaird, hacking his merry way through his ninth and last FA Cup final, could deny the lower-class northerners.

"It were a reet good day," said Olympic half-back and trainer Jack Hunter in response to an unfeasibly long question from Lord Garth Of Crook in't bar after the game.

Do not disturb
Arbroath keeper sleeps through Bonny 36-0 thrashing

Arbroath are now a rubbish lower division Scottish league side but their many centenarian fans have always got the memory of that glorious day 118-ish years ago when they thrashed mighty Bon Accord 36–0.

Yes, on 5 September 1885, just seven years after their formation, the Arbroath team set a goalscoring record for a first-class British match. Bon Accord played in their working clothes, didn't have a pair of boots between them and replaced their injured keeper with a half-back who'd never played in goal before... yes, they were a crack unit.

Arbroath winger John Petrie top-scored with 13 goals while their keeper didn't touch the ball once in 90 minutes of highly competitive first-class football.

In fact, the goalie had such an anonymous game that it was said that afterwards no-one could remember his name. Not even him. But it is possible we've made that bit up...

Women play football. No, really!
Football authorities condemn female footie farrago

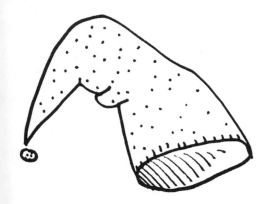

In modern times, it's unthinkable for women to play football, so imagine the shock of FA bigwigs back in the olden days of 1895 when a British Ladies Football Club was formed! These unhinged fillies played their first match at Crouch End in North London. Kitted out in big, heavy skirts, home-made shinguards and nightcaps (for some reason) they belted the pig's bladder around the park in front of a mere 10,000 spectators. Clearly, there was no interest in such a distasteful event and bewhiskered FA chiefs with their customary wisdom and foresight dismissed the game as a "farce". It is only due to their vision that the fairer sex no longer embarrass themselves in this way.

The descent of man
Darwenian theory in practice

In Darwinian theory, the game of life is really just one long battle for survival where only the strongest survive. But in 1898/99 Darwenian players at Lancashire team Darwen strived heroically to prove themselves the weakest in the game of league football.

In 1899, the Lancastrian Darwenians spectacularly achieved their noble aim, finishing bottom of the Second Division (which was the lowest division in those them there days) with an exceptional nine

points from 34 games played. They amassed one point from 17 away fixtures, scoring six and leaking 109 goals in the process. Even Loughborough, the second crappiest team in the league, couldn't descend to anywhere near Darwen's level, smashing them 10–0. Despite the fact that Darwen's games guaranteed goal action, amazingly they weren't re-elected to the League the following season. One Darwen player almost certainly remarked sadly, "We just haven't evolved as a team."

Ah, the Tartan Army... passionate, proud and, um, pink. Or at least they were for this Scotland–England encounter. Somehow, crimson-faced Derby-winning racehorse owner Lord Rosebery, who was attending the match, persuaded the Scottish FA to make his team play in his racing colours of primrose and rose (in other words, yellow and pink).

Can you imagine, burly Scottish blokes wearing pink? The next thing you know, they'll be wearing skirts... er, oh.

Having done the trick for Lord Rosebery's horse, it didn't appear to do the Scottish players any harm either as they romped to a 4–1 victory including a hat-trick from the only amateur in their side: centre-forward R.S. McColl.

"Scotland the brave? You have to be brave to wear those colours"

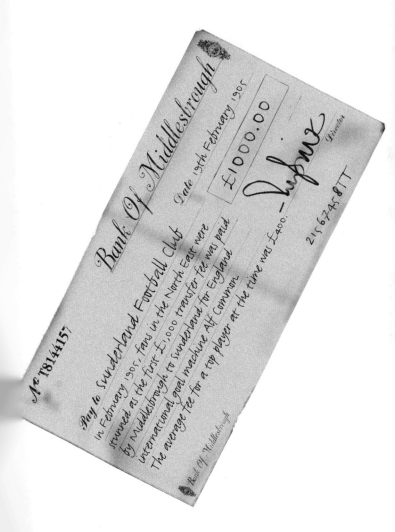

Æo T8144157

Bank Of Middlesbrough

Date 19th February 1905

£1000.00

Director

215 6745 8TT

Pay to Sunderland Football Club

In February 1905, fans in the North East were stunned as the first £1,000 transfer fee was paid by Middlesbrough to Sunderland for England international goal machine Alf Common. The average fee for a top player at the time was £400.

Bank Of Middlesbrough

United outcasts cast back in
FA suspend militant Man United stars but player power prevails

Today, of course, the FA and Manchester United enjoy a harmonious relationship that is the envy of all. No arguments about releasing players for international duty, public spats with the Reds' boss, nothing. But in August 1909, the FA suspended the whole United team!

The United players had been instrumental in forming the first players' union and at first every professional in the country signed up to join. But pressure from FA officials led to players dropping out one after the other until the Old Trafford "Outcasts" stood alone.

United had just won their first FA Cup, but it seemed the very FA whose very FA trophy they had just won would not let them play in the 1909/10 season!

Then Everton player Tim Coleman joined the Outcasts. Soon his Toffee team-mates and then loads of other teams walked out too until the Outcasts became, um, Incasts and the FA were cast out! Eventually, the FA backed down, agreement was reached and so the seeds of long-time harmony were sown…

"We only said we wanted another striker. Now we've got 11…"

West Auckland win "World Cup"!

It were a miner miracle!

How could a team of "sheep-shearers" win an international competition that hadn't been invented yet? Well, West Auckland weren't from a city in a land near land down under, they were an amateur team of "plucky miners" from a County Durham village. And the "World Cup", as it was wrongly named, was staged in Turin at Easter, 1909, by British tea merchant Sir Thomas Lipton to celebrate himself being made a Knight Of The Grand Order Of Italy (what's wrong with "The Lipton Cup", eh?). Surprisingly, the FA wouldn't send the England team, so Lipton invited the "next best team", West Auckland, who happened to be third from bottom of the Northern Amateur league.

The miraculous miners beat Red Star Zurich (like Red Star Belgrade, only better), Stuttgart and then Juventus 2–0 in't final to become champions of the "world".

And to prove it were no fluke the lamp-helmetted heroes went back to Italy the following season and defended their title!

With the First World War raging on, the 1915 FA Cup final was played out in wet and gloomy conditions at Old Trafford. A 50,000 crowd, including thousands of servicemen dressed in khaki uniform, watched Sheffield United beat Chelsea 3–0 in perhaps the most depressing Cup final ever. Match over, the crowd dispersed and went back to the business of war. And there is no punchline.

Goodwill to all men
Brits and Germans play football in No Man's Land

After four months of muddy, bloody warfare, the last thing you expect to see is the enemy putting up Christmas trees decorated with candles by their trenches!

At first, British soldiers at the Ypres Salient front thought it was a trick, but it was Christmas Eve, 1914, and soon they realized their German foes were simply up for a Yuletide celebration.

Eventually, the two sides set aside their weapons and shook hands in No Man's Land. Thus began an amazing unofficial truce that lasted for several days (to the dismay of commanding officers).

The Brits soon discovered they shared a common love with our previously hated enemy: football. A member of the Bedfordshire regiment produced a ball and soldiers from both sides had a kickabout that became the stuff of legend. Mind you, no-one has ever owned up to the errant game-ending pass that saw the ball deflate on barbed wire.

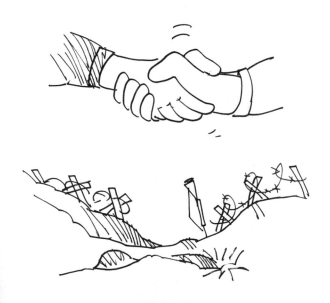

Sale of the century!

In October 1919, Leeds City players were auctioned off as the club was expelled from the league for irregular payments during the war. Managers flocked from all over the country hoping for a bargain. This is an alleged extract from the alleged auction brochure...

LEEDS CITY PLAYER AUCTION
EVERYONE MUST GO!

Hotel Metropole, Leeds   Auctioneer: Mr P Ridsdale

Lot 1   A Smith
Fiery young centre-forward who actually cares whether Leeds City win or lose. Deserves better than to be stuck with this shower. Doesn't score many goals. Purple lips.
Reserve price: £500

Lot 2   J Morris
Short midfielder. Prone to off-field trouble. You'd be mad to buy him. But we did.
Reserve price: £23

Lot 3   S Johnson
Midfielder. Average passer, average tackler, average dribbler. Really average. Hugely overpriced.
Reserve price: £5,000

Lot 4   H Kewell
Gifted dribbler with a penchant for humiliating opposing defenders and scoring spectacular goals.
Reserve price: £1,250
(but we will accept a ridiculously low offer)

Lot 5   D Batty
Experienced and trustworthy midfielder. So old he plays in carpet slippers, but leads by example. Do not let him take a penalty. Ever.
Reserve price: £300

Lot 6   M Viduka
Suspiciously fat-looking centre-forward, but lethal when he can be bothered. Which isn't often.
Reserve price: A$1,100

Mountie to the rescue

How PC Scorey and his shiny white horse saved the
1923 FA Cup final. In his own plodding words...

POLICE REPORT

Name	PC Scorey
Date	Saturday May 1923
Incident	Overcrowding in Wembley area

I mounted my horse Billy and proceeded to
trot around the vicinity of Wembley whereupon
it came to our attention that a large gathering
of people had gathered. Preliminary enquiries
revealed they were there to witness the final
game in an Association Football competition
called the Football Association Challenge Cup to
be contested by clubs named Bolton Wanderers
and West Ham United.

The venue for this match was Wembley
Stadium, the building of which had been
completed just four days previously.

The British Empire Exhibition authorities who
organized the aforementioned match have
since recorded an official attendance of
126,047. However, I witnessed thousands more
scaling the perimeter walls and entering the
ground without authorization. My own head
count would suggest that approximately
247,352 people entered the stadium.

With the assistance of other mounted
officers and the cooperation of the general
public, we proceeded to clear the pitch so the
game could commence. Bolton won 2–0.
I had kippers for supper.

Offside! Or is it... ?
One-word rule alteration causes goal glut

In 1925, a rule change of one-word proportions occurred that shook the football world to its very proportions!

Since the Great War, the beautiful game had been blighted by dullards like Newcastle United who started playing an "offside trap". An attacking player had to have at least three – count 'em, three – opposing players between him and the goal when the ball was played to him, so it was easy to catch him out. It was like watching Arsenal under George Graham – it was that bad.

When the word "three" was changed to "two" in the rule, more goals were scored literally overnight as defenders cluelessly blundered about. 6,373 goals were scored in the Football League in 1925/26, up from 4,700 in 1924/25.

Goal-mongous!

"Oh, darling, I still don't understand that dashed offside law."

Mighty atom strikes!
Pocket-sized Patsy somersaults to glory

The 1925 Scottish Cup final between Celtic and Dundee will forever be remembered for Celtic star Patsy "The Mighty Atom" Gallagher's wonder goal.

With Dundee leading 1–0 and just 15 minutes to go, "Mighty Atom" fizzed and whirled into a crowded penalty area with the ball at his feet. Just a few feet and inches from goal, a crunching tackle stopped him in his fizzy tracks. But the Cadbury's Miniature-sized shooting star atomic creature would not be denied, somehow keeping the ball lodged between his feet and somersaulting into the net with it.

Inspired by pocket Patsy's acrobatics, Celtic went on to win 2–1 and chalk up a record 11th Scottish Cup win. Atomic Kitten!

Hip to be square

The first radio broadcast of a match...
and a new phrase is born!

1

Back in the day when televised matches and no-one playing on a Saturday afternoon any more was still just a twinkle in Rupert Murdoch's eye...

4

7

2

5

...someone came up with the bright idea of broadcasting the commentary from a football match on the radio (or wireless, as it might have still been called then)...

8

3

6

...The first game chosen for this experiment was a match between Arsenal and Sheffield United on 22 January 1927. However, broadcasters were worried...

9

10

...that listeners wouldn't
be able to follow the
action. So the *Radio Times*
(back when its name
made more sense)
printed a diagram of a
pitch divided into
numbered squares...

11

...One commentator
would then describe the
action while another
called out the number of
the square so listeners
would know where the
action was taking place...

12

13

14

15

...and that's where
the phrase "Back to
square one" comes from!
Now wasn't that
educational?

Dai-day at Wembley

Welsh team win FA Cup!

They were singing atop Snowdon and baking Welsh cakes in the valleys (possibly) after Cardiff City beat Arsenal 1–0 in the 1927 FA Cup final. It was the, um, first time in a row that the FA Cup had been taken out of England and the Taffy invaders were jubilant.

Ironically, the winning goal for Cardiff was scored by Scottish-sounding Hughie Ferguson and conceded by Arsenal's Welsh-sounding Welsh international keeper Dan Lewis. Lewis let Fergie's weak shot spill out of his hands and over the line, and Welsh football history would never be the same again. Because now it was different!

The joy of six-ty
Dixie Dean goes goal ker-razy

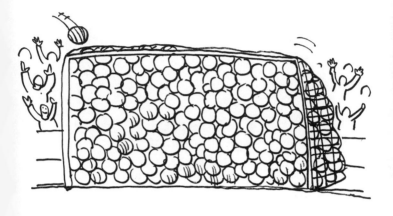

Who ever looked after the record books in the 1920s must have used an awful lot of sticky tape. A year after George Camsell had torn up the goalscoring stats, Everton's Dixie Dean shredded them again in the 1927/28 season when he overhauled Camsell's 59 league goals in a campaign by going one better and hitting 60. He left it late though, needing a hat-trick from his final match. After hitting two in the first half against Arsenal, he had to wait until eight minutes from time to get the decisive 60th – a far post header. "Trixie Dixie gets to sixty," said the headlines next day. We reckon.

Achtung Zeppelin!

FA Cup final interrupted by surprise appearance of German airship

The 1930 FA Cup final could have been remembered as the day the formerly-inspired-by-Herbert-Chapman Huddersfield were beaten by the now-inspired-by-Herbert-Chapman Arsenal, who went on to dominate British football for a decade. It could also have been remembered as the day the Cup saw one of its cleverest goals – a snappily taken one-two free kick between Alex James and Cliff Bastin. But it isn't. No, it's remembered as the day a bloody great Graf Zeppelin floated over the Twin Towers in the middle of a match. A portent of things to come midway between two wars, spectators didn't know whether to boo or cheer. Reports that the Zep flew off when the Germans realized it was "ze boring, boring Arsenal playing" cannot be confirmed…

Faint-ly ludicrous
First World Cup leaves at least one man fuming...

In 1930, Uruguay hosted (and won) the first World Cup. England, in their wisdom, didn't attend. ("It'll never catch on…").

However the United States team, which largely comprised former Scottish and English professionals, did reach a semi-final against Argentina. During which, an over-excited US medic tried to complain to the referee about something (possibly his side being 6–1 down) and accidentally broke a bottle of chloroform. The poor chap was overcome by the fumes and had to be stretchered off. The victorious Uruguayans presumably thought the whole event was a gas…

Your number's up...

Numbered shirts make their debut

The 1932/33 FA Cup campaign has two claims to fame. The second of which is that it ended with the first final where numbered shirts were worn: Everton wore numbers one (their goalkeeper) to 11, and Manchester City sported 12 to 22 (their goalkeeper).

Everton emerged victorious (and presumably happy and glorious) after goals from Stein, Dunn and that man Dixie Dean again. It gave the Merseysiders a hat-trick of success: the Second Division crown in 1931, the First Division title in 1932 and now the FA Cup...

… but long after the final, people were still talking about the third round and Third Division fodder Walsall's astonishing 2–0 victory over the footballing "royalty" that was Arsenal. The match was built up as the Bank of England team (the Arsenal side had cost some £30,000) versus the little team that cost £69.

After a brutal smash and grab (five Walsall players could have been sent off in the first 15 minutes, such was their, ahem, committed style of play), the Bank of England had been well and truly robbed.

Mutch ado about nothing
The hat-eating penalty that never was

The 1938 FA Cup final between Preston and Huddersfield had been a fairly drab affair until the final few seconds of extra time. With the score 0–0 and a goal never looking to be on the cards, BBC radio commentator Tom Woodroofe even promised listeners: "If they score now I'll eat my hat." Uh-oh Tom.

Approximately one second after his utterance, Preston's George Mutch was tackled just outside the box. Except, in these pre-Specsavers days, the referee decided it was just inside the box and awarded a penalty.

Mutch, who'd been knocked out by the challenge admitted afterwards: "I didn't even understand that a penalty had been awarded. They handed me the ball and I placed it automatically. As I took my run-up I wondered what I was doing and why. I don't remember aiming at the goal."

He was so groggy, he almost missed, but the ball just bounced over the line after coming off the crossbar.

Tom bought a new hat...

Win or die!
War looms as Mussolini, erm, encourages Italy to
World Cup victory

The year 1938 wasn't the happiest. Spain was in the throes of Civil War,
Mussolini's Italy had invaded Abyssinia and Hitler's Germany had annexed
Austria. This was the background to the World Cup finals in France (to
be the last finals for a dozen years). Italy went on to win the tournament
after rumours that Mussolini had sent them a threatening telegram on
matchday. Quite unbelievably, we have managed to obtain that telegram...

Ufficio Telegrafico di ROMA
T E L E G R A M M A

Indicazioni d'urgenza

Circuito sul quale si deve fare
l'inoltro del telegramma

```
***CIAO EVERYBODY STOP HOPE YOU ARE WELL STOP
I'M FINE STOP WEATHER IS GOOD STOP I CAN SEE
THE CAMPAIGN HERE IN ABYSSINIA IS GOING WELL
FROM MY HOTEL ROOM STOP GOOD LUCK IN THE FINAL
STOP WIN OR DIE STOP LOVE AND KISSES M
```

The world at war
The season comes to a premature end

On 2 September 1939, Blackpool were top of the First Division, the only team with maximum points. Just below them were Arsenal, who'd just beaten Sunderland 5–2, with Ted Drake scoring four. It was shaping up to be an exciting campaign. But there would in fact be no more league football for seven seasons.

"Maximum points, top of the league, this is our yea… oh bugger."

Both sides now
Stan's the man... for the hosts and the visitors

an unusual display of sportsmanship, on 25 September 1943, at Wembley,
gland allowed their twelfth man Stan Mortensen to go on as a sub for
ales as the visitors had no spare players after Ivor Powell got injured.
rhaps the generosity was a sign of confidence from the hosts. If so, it
as justified as England ran out 8–3 winners. If only England could have
rsuaded Wales to return the favour with Ryan Giggs…

Sunderland slope off
Giant killers Yeovil upset the odds again

After beating Second Division Bury in the third round of the 1948/49 FA Cup, giant killers Yeovil from the Southern League added the First Division scalp of mighty Sunderland in the fourth round. The Somerset club and their infamous sloping pitch played host to the visitors from the North-East with few expecting anything but a Sunderland victory. And when Yeovil's keeper was hurt in training and had to be replaced by solicitor's clerk Dickie Dyke (one previous senior appearance) the astronomical odds against them increased by the size of several planets (roughly).

Just 10 minutes into the match, Yeovil's winger Hargreaves pulled a muscle, becoming a virtual passenger for the rest of the game. By now the odds were scientifically proven to be too large to calculate on any known calculator.

The only player in the Yeovil team with any League experience was their player-manager Alec Stock, who described his two roles as "violent exercise on top of a pile of worries". But it was Sunderland who were worrying after Stock smacked in a goal from the edge of the box. They were a bit less worried when Robinson got them an equalizer but even more worried than they had been before when, in extra time, Bryant put Yeovil back in the lead. And then the ref blew the final whistle and Sunderland weren't worried any more. They were just sad.

American strife
England humiliated in the World Cup by the USA

Despite being joint favourites, with Brazil, going into the 1950 World Cup finals, England (yes, we'd finally agreed to participate in the thing) were embarrassed by a 1–0 defeat by the United States and the players would have come home with their tails between their legs if they'd had tails.

Neither they nor the English press pack stayed on to watch the deciding match in which Brazil lost to Uruguay before 199,854 fans.

However, American disinterest in the sport meant the victory over England barely merited any column inches at all. As this, ahem, authentic cutting from the time illustrates...

Wizard of the dribble
The Stanley Matthews Cup final

Back in 1953, the world's most famous footballer didn't wear sarongs, change his hairstyle every five minutes or have a pop star wife. But despite not bringing out an autobiography every Christmas, Stanley Matthews (yes, that's who we're talking about) was incredibly popular. So popular in fact that, come the Cup final that year, the whole country was willing him and the rest of the Blackpool team on. Well, apart from Bolton fans, who presumably wanted their team to

Matthews starts here...

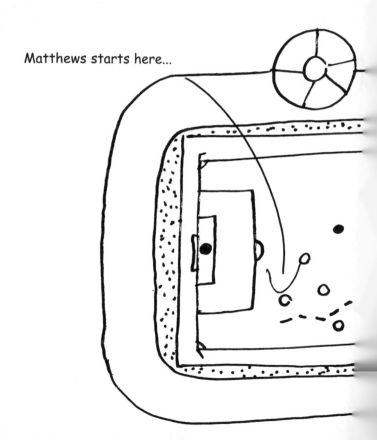

win. With two previous Cup outings ending in failure, many believed this was Stanley's last chance for a medal. And with 55 minutes gone, it wasn't looking too good: Bolton were 3–1 up. Yikes! Fortunately, an irresistible Matthews led the recovery with a series of superb, mazy runs down the wing, inspiring Blackpool to an epic recovery and 4–3 win.

A nation rejoiced and Stanley didn't even feel the need to write a book about it. Hooray!

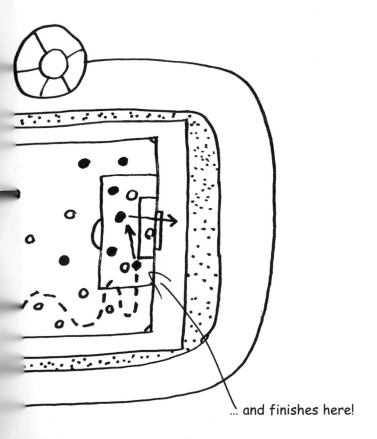

... and finishes here!

37 Home truths
England get a lesson in modern football at Wembley

It had always been assumed, well by the English anyway, that the best nation in the world at football were... well, England of course. But on a brisk November afternoon at Wembley in 1953 Hungary's "Magical Magyars" dismantled that cosy notion. Not only did they inflict England's first home defeat by continental opposition, they ran riot, demolishing the hosts 6–3 and putting paid to any lingering thoughts of superiority with their vastly more polished display.

The Times summed up the mood of the nation when it reported: "Yesterday, the inevitable happened. England at last were beaten by the foreign invader." Ouch.

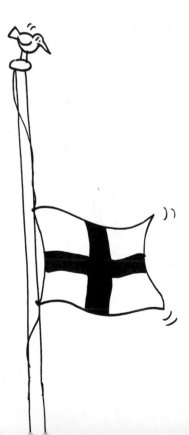

38 Injury time
Cup final keeper plays on with a broken neck

People handle pain in different ways. Some are hysterical, some bravely stoic. And some, like Bert Trautmann, are completely bloody oblivious to it. The Manchester City goalkeeper was playing in the 1956 FA Cup final when, with 15 minutes left, he dived at the feet of Birmingham's Peter Murphy. He got up, dazed and reeling, but to the crowd's chorus of "For he's a jolly good fellow," carried on playing as his side won 3–1.

Three days later, after complaining of "headaches", X-rays revealed he had in fact broken his neck and one too-firm pat on the back could have killed him. Safe to say from then on no-one ever accused Bert of being a drama queen...

"Now Mr Trautmann, let's have a look at you... Argh!"

The beautiful game
Brazil rule and Pele becomes a household name

Edson Arantes do Nascimento was only 17 when he came to the World Cup finals in Sweden in the summer of 1958. Pele, the name by which he was equally unknown, made his debut in Brazil's third qualifying game, against the Soviet Union. Three matches and six Pele goals later, Brazil were world champions and Pele was a household name.

The Brazilians were simply in a different class to Europe's finest, whom they made look more pedestrian than a zebra crossing full of penguins (or something), with better tactics and unbelievable skills. There was a new football world order and Brazil were, very clearly, at the top of it.

"If only we could sell personalised replica shirts, we'd make a fortune."

What a load of rubbish
Angry fans pelt 1960 FA Cup winners Wolves with garbage

You win the greatest club cup competition in the world; you collect the famous FA Cup from a royal dignitary; you parade around the pitch in front of cheering fans doing silly dances and taking turns to put the trophy lid on your head... it's every footballer's dream. But in 1960, victorious Wolves players had to use the famous trophy as a shield as angry Blackburn Rovers fans pelted them with apple cores and orange peel (they didn't have frankfurters and M&Ms back in the olden days).

The match had been totally rubbish and hinged on an unlucky injury to Blackburn left-back Dave Whelan, who broke his leg trying to tackle Wolves' Norman Deeley after half an hour when the score was just 1–0 to Wolves.

As no substitutes were yet allowed 10-man Rovers succumbed to a 3–0 defeat, with Deeley scoring twice in the second-half using his unbroken legs. Frustrated by the Wolves players' fierce tackling and the inaction of Kevin Howley (the youngest man to referee a Cup final), Rovers fans threw rubbish during the traditional lap of honour causing the media to dub the shame game the "Dustbin Final".

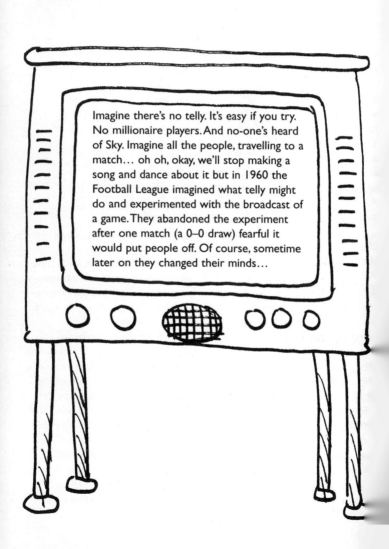

Imagine there's no telly. It's easy if you try. No millionaire players. And no-one's heard of Sky. Imagine all the people, travelling to a match... oh oh, okay, we'll stop making a song and dance about it but in 1960 the Football League imagined what telly might do and experimented with the broadcast of a game. They abandoned the experiment after one match (a 0–0 draw) fearful it would put people off. Of course, sometime later on they changed their minds...

"The Chin" saves the day: Part 1
Players and authorities clash but Jimmy prevails

Player power, 'eh? Long before England players were allegedly threatening to strike over drug test shenanigans there was an even bigger threat of strike action.

In 1961, players were getting tired of the deal surrounding their wages and contracts. They were restricted to a maximum salary of £20 – far less than they could earn abroad. And they weren't allowed to move to a club of their choosing when their contract expired. A "slave contract," Jimmy Hill called it.

Yes, he of the remarkable chinnage was the chairman of the Professional Footballers Association at the time and threatened to bring his members out on strike if changes weren't forthcoming.

When the strike was called for January 21, the League insisted all clubs move their games to the 20th to avoid it. "What way to run a sport," jeered the *Daily Mirror* in an editorial entitled "Idiotic!"

Fortunately, the League backed down and Chinny prevailed. Football had been dragged out of the Dark Ages and there would never be any rows again… (What's that? Oh, okay, scrap that last bit).

Lawman swamped
Denis Law's six-goal haul is washed out

The 1960/61 FA Cup fourth round tie between Manchester City and Luton Town at Kenilworth Road turned into Swan Lake with boots (sort of) as torrential rain reduced the pitch to a mushy-pea-like bog. Luton squelched into a 2–0 lead within 15 minutes before balletic City striker Denis Law proved he could walk, dribble and score on water!

While all around him sloshed and slithered, twinkle-toes Law fired in six goals. But with City 6–2 up and 21 minutes remaining, the referee must have decided his socks were getting a little *too* uncomfortably wet and abandoned the game. In the rematch, luckless Law scored again but City were sunk 3–1 by the lucky Luton.

"Och, c'mon, ref. It's still playable."

Stan's pulling power
Matthews makes triumphant return to Stoke

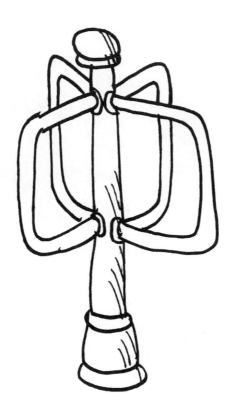

Some players simply put bums on seats (er, or at least, feet on terraces). Stanley Matthews was such a player. In 1961, when the 5-year-old Matthews returned to Stoke City after a 14-year absence (he'd been playing for Blackpool), the club attendance shot up from 8,000 to 35,000 in the space of one game. Which made his Stoke team-mates particularly happy — they received a bonus of £1 for every thousand fans attending over the 12,000 mark.

In for a pound...

Greavesie becomes Britain's most expensive player

After just a few unhappy months spent in Italy, Jimmy Greaves returned to British football in December 1961, for a record transfer fee when Tottenham spent £99,999 to buy him from Milan. The Spurs manager Bill Nicholson deliberately made the fee one pound short of six figures because he didn't want Greaves to feel pressurized by being the first £100,000 footballer.

The striker certainly didn't seem too stressed – he scored a hat-trick on his debut.

HALF-TIME

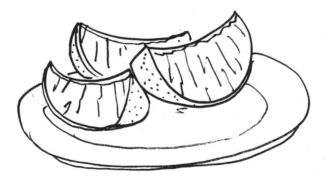

The big chill
Flamin' hell, it was freezing!

It was cold, the winter of 1962/63. So cold that even more football matches than normal were postponed. In fact, after Christmas the football authorities were starting to get really rather worried. On 5 January, only three of the 32 FA Cup third round matches could take place and just a handful of league games. The following week it was even worse with only eight matches in the country going ahead. Soon, some matches had been delayed and re-arranged more than 10 times.

Eventually, the season had to be extended by several weeks. But not before clubs had tried some bizarre solutions to beat the freeze. Leicester put a tent over their pitch, but Blackpool went the furthest – employing a flame thrower in the vain hope of softening up their pitch.

It didn't work but we suspect there must be a "the season was really hotting up" gag in there somewhere...

The price of glory
Can money really buy the title?

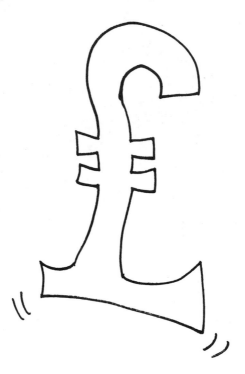

Blue shirts, cheque book at the ready. No not the current set-up at Chelsea. This was back in those more "innocent" times, the Sixties. Although perhaps it was only the prices that differed. Having spent £175,000 on new players the previous season, Everton proceeded to pay another £100,000 on a couple more to make a challenge for the 1963 League championship. It paid off as the Merseysiders cruised to the title although critics labelled them "cheque book champions". The celebratin Evertonians didn't seem too upset though…

The twelfth man
League finally allows substitutes

After years of 10-man sides, the League finally decided that from the start of the 1965/66 season, teams would be allowed to have one substitute on the bench who could come on to replace of an injured player. Which, given some of the, ahem, "challenges" that still passed for tackles, was probably a good idea.

"He says it was his own number 12 who kicked him..."

What's the difference?
A tale of broken Hearts

Sometimes, it's the little things that matter. Like goal difference. Or goal average as it was back in 1965. (Now, stick with us because this next bit is complicated.)

On the final day of the Scottish season, Kilmarnock beat Hearts 2–0. This meant both clubs had played 34 games, won 22, drawn six and lost six. But Hearts had scored 90 and conceded 49 goals, whilst Kilmarnock had scored 62 and conceded 33. On goal *average* (remember, that was the method of the day) that made Kilmarnock champions, and so they were. But

a bitterly disappointed Hearts pointed out that if matters had been settled on goal *difference*, they would have won the title.

Hearts demanded the rules were changed, and the League agreed – from the following season. Which wasn't much consolation to Hearts fans.

As a somewhat ironic postscript, some 21 years later Hearts were pipped to the title by Celtic – on goal difference. If the old method of goal average had still applied, it would have been Hearts instead who were champions. Doh!

Viva El Beatle!
Bestie gets the Fab Four treatment

Isn't Georgie Best just the fabbest?!
Those crazy Benfica fans certainly think
so. They got hip to him the moment he
took a stroll through their pad in 1966 with
his mop top and his rubber soles and
scored two goals in 12 minutes. Georgie
and his Manchester United mates ended
up 5-1 winners and Benfica were no
longer toppermost of the poppermost.
After the game, Georgie was mobbed to
cries of "El Beatle" and one fan even tried
to cut off a lock of his hair. Georgie took it
all in his stride and flew back to Blighty
with a smile like a sunbeam and wearing
a sombrero. Why the hip hat GB?
"I dunno, I just wanted a souvenir," says
Georgie Boy. Far out!

Stop! Thief! Woof!

Dog gets the FA out of a pickle

It's not really what you want, is it? A few months before you're about to host the World Cup and suddenly the trophy goes missing.

The FA was suitably embarrassed when it transpired that the Jules Rimet trophy, left in Central Hall, Westminister, had been stolen. The thief didn't take the stamps that were also in the hall. A shame for him as they were worth some £3 million (the World Cup was only worth about £3,000).

The thief was never caught but the trophy was discovered a week later by a dog named Pickles in some bushes in Norwood, south London. Although, thinking about it, it was probably his owner who phoned the authorities.

Champions of the world
England's wingless wonders come good

The 1966 World Cup final. And one question remains unanswered: did it cross the line? The Germans said "No", we said, "Yea… ooh!" and Backhramov the Russian linesman said "Yes" (hey, we were going to say yes too, we were just thinking about it first, that's all, honest).

All that matters is that Geoff Hurst's second goal, and England's third, counted.

Even before that drama there had already been plenty of thrills (and, hey, maybe even some spills). West Germany took the lead after 12 minutes through Haller. Hurst equalized six minutes later. England gained the advantage in the 78th minute after Peters struck home and then Germany heart-breakingly got a late equalizer through Weber seconds before the whistle.

Extra time could have gone either way. "You've beaten them once, now do it again," was Alf Ramsey's advice. "Look at them, they're finished!" (He wasn't a man of many words, Alf.)

Alan Ball found some extra pace in his tired legs, crossed the ball to Hurst who turned and smashed it against the underside of the bar and down onto the line… but did it cross that line?

The record books say yes and Hurst put the result beyond doubt in the final seconds. Blimey, England had won the World Cup!

Jock's bhoys quad joy!

Jock Stein's Celtic do the Quadruple!

There was a day when a Scottish team stood astride European football like a really big colossus. That day was the 1966/67 season, and that team was Celtic, and that Celtic was managed by Jock Stein.

After winning all three domestic competitions, Jock's team of Bhoys headed for Lisbon to try and become the first British team ever to win the European Cup.

The apocryphal script for the final said that classy opponents Inter Milan would finally expose the, well, crapness of Scottish football. But canny Jock took that Italian script and wrote another fundamentally more Scottish one.

He made sure his players were so relaxed they were singing songs in the tunnel before the game, which, like, totally freaked out the Italians.

Then big Jock upstaged the great Inter coach Helenio Herrera by sitting on the bench Herrera had earmarked for himself, and refusing to budge.

What remained of that original script was completely shredded when goals by Tommy Gemmell and Steve Chalmers gave Celtic a 2–1 win. The Bhoys had won the Quad!

54 Sealed with a (Millwall) kiss
Wolf man KO'd by 'Wall man

There's nothing like the thrill of a last-minute goal to spark a joyous pitch invasion. And when Wolves striking legend Derek Dougan scored a last-gasp equalizer in a Second Division match against Millwall in April 1967, it was nothing like a joyous pitch invasion.

Happy Wolf "The Doog" turned to celebrate with a supporter who'd run on the pitch, only belatedly to deduce that it was an angry Millwall fan. The clue was probably in the fact that the fan punched him in the face…

Don't walk!
New ruling forces keepers to keep in step

Season 1967/68 was a sad one for guardians of the onion bag as the International Football Board introduced a new rule limiting goalkeepers to four steps while holding the ball before releasing it into play. Thus spectators were denied the thrilling spectacle of goalies zig-zagging across their penalty area trampling on valuable grass and chewing up seconds of essential playing time.

A goalkeeper we would have spoken to at the time if we hadn't just made him up was outraged: "It's an absolute infringement of my human rights. Some of my happiest minutes are spent carrying a ball round the penalty area while opposition centre-forwards try to kick me up the arse." Strangely, no-one listened.

Pat sticks one in the onion bag
Shot-stopper shoots and scores in Charity Shield thriller

Traditionally, Charity Shield matches are dishwater dull, but one mighty punt by Tottenham Hotspur keeper Pat Jennings added Fairy Liquid froth to the 1967 game, a 3–3 thriller between Spurs and Manchester United at Old Trafford.

Big Pat, whose shovel-like hands made a football look like a ping-pong ball, showed he also had big feet when he sent a huge kick upfield from the edge of the Spurs penalty area.

A high wind (and perchance a little puff from Mother Nature?) sent the ball swirling over Spurs forwards and United defenders, before bouncing over the tortured head of a furiously back-pedalling United keeper Alex Stepney and into the goal.

"I couldn't believe it," laughed big punter Pat afterwards. "I wasn't even sure it counted in the laws of the game."

Well Pat, it did.

The Yo-Yo club

When they were up, they were up, and when they were down, they were down...

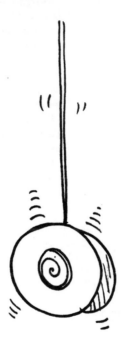

Yo, yo, yo, YO! In 1969, Northampton Town completed a dizzying yo-y ride from the Fourth Division to the First Division and back down again. Town's phoenix-like rise from the ashes began in 1960. Within five seasons they were sucking up oxygen in the highest altitudes of English football. They really sucked though, and it took them just four seasons to splashland in the heap of Fourth Division ashes from whence they had, er, hitherto risen.

Football starts war!

Fiery Honduras-El Salvador World Cup encounter ends badly

When some over-excited Sky presenter hypes up a handbags-at-dawn clash between Joey Barton (probably) and A.N. Other contender, you might think football's turned into some kind of warzone. But back in 1969, it really did! Yes, the (deep breath) World Cup Central & North American Zone qualifying group semi-final tie between El Salvador and Honduras actually sparked a full-scale war between the two countries.

The two-legged tie was level after both legs, so they had to play a decider. Crowd riots at all three games provoked running battles along the Honduras–El Salvador border. El Salvador finally prevailed 3–2 in the deciding game.

Rather than exchange the traditional polite end-of-game handshakes, the two countries opted instead to break off diplomatic relations. A fortnight later El Salvador invaded Honduras. It was war!

In the summer of 1970, UEFA
decreed that matches that finished
all-square in their European
competitions would no longer be
decided by the toss of a coin, but
by the test of nerve and skill that
is the penalty shoot-out.

On 3 September 1970, Gareth
Southgate was born.

Clodoaldo, Tostao, Rivelino, Jairzinho, Pele-o... the names of Brazil's 1970 World Cup-winning stars slip off the tongue as smoothly as Castrol GTX (kids, don't try that at home).

Brazil steamrollered dullards Italy 4–1 in the final in Mexico City, but the *real* final was their group match against the mighty Three Lions in Guadalajara: Banksie's save from Pele (flip reversed in mid-air, wasn't it?); Jairzinho's winning goal (Tostao beats three, passes to Pele, pops it to Jairzinho and it's a gooooooooooaaaalllll!); Jeff Astle's infamous miss (ooh!); Mooro and Pele exchanging shirts at the end (aah!)... it was the beautiful game at its Brazil-nuts-for goalposts most beautiful. Marvellous.

Mooro thunderbolt KOs ref!
West Ham and England legend blows whistle on groggy ref

Bobby Moore: a name synonymous with sportsmanship, dignity and all that is good about English football. Born with an innate ability to read the game, Mooro was always a couple of yards ahead of the average footballer in his head and on grass… even when he was knocking out referees!

During a game for West Ham v Wolves on 14 November 1970, Mooro's thunderous clearance scored a direct hit on the man in black, knocking him unconscious. Quick-thinking Bobby, who'd scored a great goal earlier in the match, immediately grabbed the prostrate ref's whistle, blew it to stop the game and called for the physio. What a man, what a mighty, mighty good man.

Strike a light!
Floodlights switched off as miners walk out

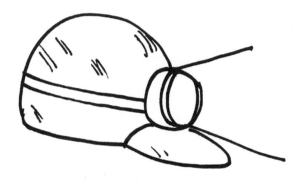

1973/74, midweek matches were suspended because of power cuts caused by the miner's strike. And as winter approached, clubs were allowed to kick off their Saturday games at 2.15pm so they finished before sunset.

Bizarrely, it was felt that powering floodlights for our glorious national game was a lower priority than heating homes or boiling an egg. Bizarre...

If only the Football Association had listened to our bright idea to invite all striking miners to watch evening games for free, they could have used their helmet lamps to illuminate the pitch. Simple.

Arm-breaker Luigi's leg broken

Ledge Luigi gets his leguppance

Between 1965 and 1974, Italian striking legend Luigi Riva bashed in a record 35 goals in 42 internationals. Renowned for his speed, courage and deadly left-foot shot, Luigi was one of Italy's best-loved players. One fan didn't love Luigi quite so much though after Luigi unleashed one of his deadly accurate shots, missed the goal by a mile and broke the fan's arm during a practice match in October 1970.

But by a bone-shattering crunch of fate, a few days later, Italy played Austria in Vienna and deadly legend Luigi was stretchered off with a broken leg. Snap!

"The Chin" saves the day: Part 2
It's that man again!

You just can't keep a good man with a protuberant chin and funny beard down! Having freed footballers from slavery back in 1961 (see moment 42), Chinny saved civilization yet again during a match between Liverpool and Arsenal at Highbury in September 1972. When a linesman got injured, "Sir" Jimmy (Saville's got a knighthood, so why no gong for Hill, eh Mr Prime Minister?) temporarily abandoned his commentator's microphone and took up the official's flag. Clearly, he was unsuited to a job that traditionally attracts know-all busy-bodies who love the sound of their own voice, but Jimmy took it all on the chin.

Clown makes fool of England
Circus entertainer tames Three Lions in one night!

All that stood between England and the 1974 World Cup finals was a circus entertainer! Before England's final qualifying match against Poland, which England needed to win, outspoken Derby manager and TV pundit Brian Clough informed the nation that the Polish goalkeeper Jan Tomaszewski was a clown.

For someone more used to slinging custard pies and squirting water out of plastic flowers, Jan proved to be a pretty handy keeper. Clearly, his training as a physical comedian stood him in good stead as he used every part of his anatomy – fist, fingertip, leg, hand, torso, wig – to repel shot after shot. He was beaten just once, by an Allan Clarke penalty, but the game finished 1–1 and England were eliminated.

Soon goalkeepers up and down the country were training in big red plastic shoes. Possibly.

Total football

Cruyff and co. make the world sit up and take notice

The best World Cups are when a team or a player does something so innovative or brilliant that every kid in the world immediately wants to repeat the trick in the playground. Which makes the 1974 World Cup a particularly fine event.

Two teams dominated. Germany, with their revolutionary sweeper system, that was sort of like the Italians but with the sweeper (the legendary Beckenbauer) starting attacks rather than just mopping up at the back. And Holland, whose equally revolutionary "Total Football" (everyone can play everywhere, orchestrated by the also-legendary Cruyff) was simply very, very exciting to watch.

In the final, Germany came out on top but Cruyff at least has the knowledge that every single kid in the world spent the next few years tying themselves in knots trying to master the "Cruyff Turn".

"Aarggh, mum!"

X-Rated action

Crackpot coppers recommend film-style match classifications

Football hooliganism. It's not big and it's not clever. Although neither were the bright sparks at the Police Superintendents Association.

During the 1975/76 season, they suggested one way to combat the growing hooliganism problem was by "rating" matches with a film-style classification. That way, people would know what to expect when they went to a game. (No, really!)

Funnily enough, the idea didn't catch on. But if it had done, and if there had been a police officer called Jonathan Woss, and if he wrote film-style previews of matches, who knows what it might have looked like…

Whether you're a fighter or a family

WOSSY'S FAMILY FAVOURITE

Isle of Skye v Isle of Eigg

Fancy a local derby without the aggro this weekend? Then why not make the short trip to the north-west of Scotland, hop on a ferry to the Isle of Eigg and witness this clash of the Titans. Mix freely with opposition fans and chat to the island's one policeman. Not many people live on Eigg so if there are injuries you might even get a game! The queue for Bovril at half-time moves fast and your kids will love the 5p sausage rolls (home-made by Mrs Auchterlogie). The football will be crap.

Wossy's rating: U

RATINGS: XXX - Bring a gun X - Extreme viole

WOSSY AT THE FOOTIE

Leeds v Manchester United

...efinitely not for the kids, but ...ard-core hoolies will relish this ...ne. Knuckledusters, knives, ...achetes, samurai swords and ...fles are often carried at this ...xture... and that's just by the ...olice. Beware of flying bricks ...nd replica Jocky Wilson darts. ...ew up jacket pockets to deter ...redatory urinators.

Wossy's rating: X

Liverpool v Everton

...ousers only - anyone who doesn't find Liverpool's "legendary Scouse wit" funny should give Anfield a wide berth. Red-Blue family feuds may escalate into full-scale slanging matches. And beware: Cilla Black has been booked to sing "You'll Never Walk Alone" at half-time!

Wossy's rating: 12

Leicester City v Derby County

Always a tasty fixture, but under-cover cop PC McIntyre (photo available on request) has infiltrated Leicester City's notorious Walkers Crispy gang and his intelligence should ensure the match goes off without going off big-style. Avoid large groups of socially inadequate, middle-aged, shaven-headed men who smell of cheeseburgers and hand grenades.

Wossy's rating: X

Millwall v Whoever they are playing

Do not go within five miles of this match. Seriously, don't. You will die.

Wossy's rating: XXX

...ans under 16 unless with an adult. 12 - Unsavoury scenes and bad language. U - Good clean family fun

FA block FA kissing ban move
Goalscorers given all-clear to get jiggy widdit

In 1975/76, the Football Association's Match Committee suggested players who "kissed and cuddled" after a goal was scored should be charged with bringing the game into disrepute.

Favouring a stiff handshake themselves, the uptight old codgers wanted to deny fans the chance to see their heroes writhing in post-goal ecstasy. Happily, other members of the FA more comfortable with their sexuality rejected the proposal as "impracticable", and players remained free to express their beautiful love any which way they pleased.

Rocket Man lands in Watford
New chairman at Vicarage Road promises lift-off

Fourth Division Watford got a rocket man-powered boost in May 1976 when multi-millionaire glam rock star and alleged astronaut Elton John became their new chairman.

"I'm really serious about this, I hope people will not treat this as a gimmick," Mr John told the assembled press as he adjusted his star-shaped spectacles and eased his platform boots under the boardroom table.

Revie sheiks on Dubai deal
England boss deserts to the desert

In July '77, dastardly England boss Don Revie shocked the nation when he defected to the desert. After winning just 14 and losing seven out of 29 internationals in three years, and with England needing a miracle to qualify for the 1978 World Cup finals, Don jumped before he was pushed.

Before formally resigning, crafty Don privately spoke to the FA and generously offered to "save trouble and go" if they paid up the rest of his contract (£50,000).

When asked if he had another job lined up, absent-mined Don said "No", forgetting that he'd already negotiated a £340,000 tax-free four-year contract to manage the United Arab Emirates. It seems that, previously, instead of going to Helsinki to scout out future World Cup qualifying opponents Italy against Finland, Don had accidentally got on a plane to Dubai instead. As you do.

After old dastard Don walked off into the golden tax-free sunset, fans expected the FA to appoint a safe, uncontroversial figure to steady the ship. Surprisingly though, they didn't give Don's old job to Brian Clough, opting instead for outspoken maverick Ron Greenwood.

Double-sided Pele says farewell

Brazilian ledge swaps teams in final match!

On 1 October 1977, arguably the greatest player of all-time (apart from Diego Maradona and John Fashanu) and the future face of Viagra, ended his 22-year career with a farewell exhibition match between Brazilian club Santos and New York Cosmos. Pele had scored 1,090 goals in 1,114 games for Santos before retiring in 1974 and then unretiring to play for the Cosmos.

Seventy-seven thousand people packed the 77,000-capacity Giants Stadium to see the future credit card salesman play the first half for New York Cosmos (scoring with a stunning free-kick) and the second half wearing the Santos number 10 shirt that he'd made famous.

If only Pele had swapped his Santos, Cosmos or Brazil shirts for an England shirt and been English throughout his career, English football history would have been very much better indeed.

"Don't worry, he's playing for your lot in the second half."

72 Jocks run amok at Wembley
Tartan terrors rip up hallowed turf

WEMBLEY
TURF
1977

Hordes of tartan-clad loons celebrated Scotland's 2–1 Home Championship-clinching win over England in 1977 with a boozy pitch invasion. The victory took their tally of wins over the Auld Enemy on English soil to a massive five since 1938, and understandably the sozzled Scots fans wanted soiled souvenirs of the occasion.

The merry mentalists gleefully set about digging up sods of turf until the goalmouths were bereft of sods, as well as cracking both crossbars and tearing down the goal nets. A total of 132 haggis-munching Wembley-wreckers were arrested that weekend and £18,000 of damage was caused, but a few living rooms in Scotland would soon display their own little piece of England.

Britain's first million quid player!

Cloughie shoves all his chips on a guy called Trevor

Nowadays, a million pounds might buy you Andy Carroll's left calf muscle, but in the Seventies you could buy three whole good players for that amount. That was until 9 February 1979, when Nottingham Forest boss Brian Clough decided to spend £1,180,000 on just one player: Birmingham City and England striker Trevor Francis. Thus a man named Trevor became Britain's first million pound player, smashing the previous transfer fee record of £500,000.

The, um, striking disadvantage of buying a striker so late in the season was that Francis would only be eligible for one match in the European Cup – the final.

Cloughie had not just put all his chips on Francis, he'd smothered them in ketchup. But his gamble paid off, because Forest made the final, Francis played and scored the winner. Pontoon!

Fergie breaks old firm duopoly

Minnows monopolize 1979/80 Scottish Championship

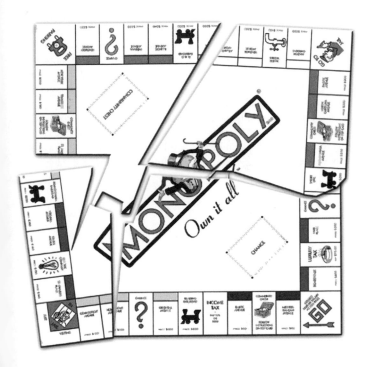

In the game of Duopoly that is Scottish football, the Old Firm of Celtic and Rangers traditionally own all the streets, houses and hotels and rarely go directly to jail without passing "Go". But in 1979/80, long-time tenants Aberdeen – managed by future knight of the realm Alex Ferguson – forcibly bought up the Old Firm's Scottish League Championship hotel. It was only the second time Aberdeen had won the title in their 77-year history and first time since 1965 that neither Celtic nor Rangers had won the league. Their Duopoly board was blasted to smithereens. For a while.

Just like the real thing
QPR replace their pitch with artificial turf

When is grass not grass? When it's astroturf. In 1981 Queens Park Rangers decided to improve on the best that Mother Nature can offer by digging up their pitch and replacing it with an all-weather artificial surface. The club saw it as a shrewd plan that would enable Loftus Road to stage other events during the week and bring in more money to the Second Division club. But, things didn't go exactly to plan. After an initially warm response players started to complain that the ball bounced unnaturally high and that any sort of sliding contact resulted in carpet burns.

Soon, QPR realized that the grass is actually greener on the other side, especially if it's, er, grass and went back to the real thing.

"You get a nice even bounce on this pitch..."

obert "Cap'n Bob" Maxwell, hailed as a hero for saving Oxford United, ecame somewhat less popular after buying a controlling interest in eading. Especially when he revealed his plan to merge the two teams to one, called Thames Valley Royals. Oxford fans staged a sit-in on the tch while a black coffin was paraded around Reading, which most servers interpeted as a sign that the fans possibly weren't happy. The erger was eventually foiled. As was the Captain's later attempt (good ef) to buy Manchester United.

"Divine" Diego
The best and worst of Maradona

England were knocked out of the 1986 World Cup by eventual winners Argentina. The South Americans first goal was actually a deliberate handball by Diego Maradona but went unpunished by what can only be described (well, by us) as short-sighted officials. TV cameras revealed the truth but the Argentinian number 10 shrugged off the incident, nonchalantly describing it as "The Hand of God".

A shell-shocked England, having witnessed the worst of Maradona, then saw the best as he waltzed embarrassingly effortlessly past almost the entire team to score a stunning solo goal. Darn.

It later transpired that God (an England fan ever since He created Saint Gary Lineker) was none too pleased to be associated with the Cheating One's goal. As another of our (cough) exclusives can exclusively reveal…

The Catholic Times

June 1986   WORLD EXCLUSIVE SPECIAL

DON'T FORCE MY HAND SAYS GOD

Big boss slams Archbishop

[WORLD EXCLUSIVE]

God today launched a scathing attack on the Archbishop of Buenos Aires designed to scath, and attack.

In an open letter, that anyone can openly read, the number one Amighty, He-who-must-be-obeyed SLAMMED Maradona for claiming use of His hand, BLASTED the Archbishop for celebrating the goal and

LAMBASTED officials for not following his instructions. The Big Cheese, currently holidaying in an exclusive hideaway with his showbiz chums Elton John and Wendy Richard, took time out from his break to pen the following missive, which was delivered on a thunderbolt to Buenos Aires Cathedral:

> Dear Bishop,
>
> Hello. How are you? I'm fine. Weather here is good. From my hotel room I have a lovely view of the beach. It's very nice (one of my better ones). Now what's this I hear that Argentinians are claiming Maradona's first goal was the, ahem "Hand of God"?
>
> I would like it publicly noted for the record that my hand was nowhere near that goal. It was here with the rest of me, getting a tan. I've never liked that Diego (apart from the "loving all mankind" thing, obviously). Why can't he use the God-given talents I gave him more appropriately. God knows what will become of him (I really do, and I can tell you – it's not pretty).
>
> Anyway, must dash. Elton's having a very glitzy barbeque and I want to get a few autographs. As I say, no more dragging me into this matter. I'm on holiday for God's sake!
>
> Best wishes
> G

The Crazy Gang
Wimbledon and their unique, er, spirit

The 1987/88 season showed both sides (or should that be cheeks?) of Wimbledon Football Club. The minnows from South London rose from obscurity to the top flight through a combination of luck, skill, determination, team spirit and, oh yes, kicking the ball very high in the air and running after it.

Their finest moment came in the 1988 FA Cup when they pulled off one of the biggest shocks ever by beating Liverpool 1–0 in the final. Peter Beardsley did actually score for Liverpool but the referee pulled play back for a Liverpool free kick. While the players were still disputing that, Lawrie Sanchez scored for the Dons.

That season the club were also charged with bringing the game into disrepute when nine of their players dropped their shorts during a testimonial game. Bums.

PC Brian
Cloughie takes the law into his own hands

Ah, Brian Clough, so much to answer for. Including on occasion taking policing matters into his own hands. In January 1989, after Nottingham Forest's 5–2 defeat of QPR in the quarter-finals of the League Cup, some fans made the foolish decision to invade the pitch.

Cloughie was having none of it. He grabbed two fans, clipped them round the ears and dragged them off the pitch. Some hailed him a hero, others felt he shouldn't have descended to their level. Cloughie apologized, as did the fans and order was restored – apart from the fact that the FA banned the Forest manager from the touchline for the rest of the season. Spoilsports.

"Don't need to go there these days… Cloughie takes care of things!"

Tears of a clown
Gazza gets it off his chest at the World Cup

The 1990 World Cup, whilst an otherwise goal-lite and cynical affair, was in fact one of England's best efforts. We reached the semi-finals inspired by, arguably, the player of the tournament, Paul Gascoigne.

The plastic boob-wearing, childishly simple Gascoigne could be an absolute idiot, as he was the first to admit, but on the pitch he was anything but a tit (most of the time).

Against Belgium in the second round, he earned England a quarter-final place. In the last minute of extra time he picked up a ball just outside the England penalty area and ran straight at the heart of the Belgian midfield. In their panic to stop him, the Belgians conceded a free-kick. Gascoigne grabbed the ball, launched it over the defence to the incoming David Platt who volleyed home.

A quarter-final against Cameroon, subsequently successfully negotiated, meant England were now only one game from the final. Of course it did involve having to face the Germans in Turin, but still, one game away!

A 1–1 draw took the match to penalties but missses from Stuart Pearce and Chris Waddle ended England's stay.

The abiding memory, though, was not the penalty misses but the sight of a tearful Gascoigne after he picked up the booking that ensured he would have missed the final, had England reached it.

The next day's newspapers, full of Gascoigne's tears, hit a nerve with the country and we welcomed him into our collective, um, bosom.

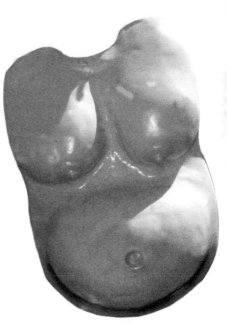

One minute you're top of the world, the next you're, well, somewhere near the scrapheap. Diego Maradona's decline came in unpleasant chunks of tabloid scandal and stupid decisions.

In 1991, he left Italy in disgrace after a drugs and sex scandal. A national opinion poll at the time found he was less popular with Italians than Saddam Hussein.

He had one more World Cup outing but was sent home from the US in disgrace after failing a drugs test. His final appearance i an Argentinian 10 was a testimon Afterwards the shirt was "retire from the national team.

Goody two boots

Saint Lineker wins award

As he came to the end of a remarkable career in 1991 (with only a brief sojourn to Japan to come), Gary Lineker was given a FIFA Fair Play award and a cheque for £20,000 for having never been booked or sent-off in his career. He collected his prize with a shrug and a smile, as a choir of angels sang beatitudes. Slowly, Gary spread his wings and flew into the light... well the lights of a TV studio for his new career as a pundit.

It's a steel!
Middlesbrough carelessly lose sponsor

The cornerstone of modern football is sponsorship. All those dull and dusty corporations believe, because of their association with the beautiful game, that we'll all buy more phones, crisps, boots, cars, umbrellas, whatever. However, they expect a little something for their cash. So when British Steel discovered that the club they were funding in the 1990s, Middlesbrough, had constructed their new £16 million stadium using only 2,000 tonnes of British steel and 18,000 tonnes imported from Germany, they were out of the door before you could say "How big do you want your name on the shirt?" Whoops.

Eric Cantona, the mercurial French striker idolized by many, despised by quite a few, had always been somewhat unpredictable. But no-one, absolutely no-one, could have expected what he did at Selhurst Park in January 1995. Having been sent off (again), Cantona was making his way along the touchline when a Palace "fan" ran screaming from his seat to share his opinions on Eric, his mother and the French race. Incensed, Cantona reacted by launching a two-footed kung-fu-style kick at the supporter. Sacre bleu! (Or maybe Hai-ya!).

A nation watched open-mouthed and Eric was subsequently banned and almost jailed.

Sometimes, as a journalist, a 0–0 draw can be a difficult match to report on. No goals to describe can leave you flailing around looking for one small incident to focus on. Just one little unusual detail... like perhaps a goalkeeper doing the most outrageous acrobatic clearance in the history of the game. Yes, England v Colombia's friendly at Wembley may have been a dull 0–0 but did you see that kick?! For some reason best known to himself, Colombia keeper Rene Higuita decided to clear a high ball by diving under it, flipping his legs behind him and scorpion-like, flicking it clear. He may have pointlessly risked conceding an embarrassing goal but in playgrounds (and offices) up and down the country people were doing themselves an injury for months after trying to repeat what they'd seen.

Money matters
The Bosman ruling makes a lot of agents rich

In 1986 a little-known Belgian player, Jean-Marc Bosman, made history and changed football forever.

Bosman was unhappy when his club RC Liege blocked his transfer to a French club after his contract had ended.

The Belgian promptly took Liege, the Belgian FA and UEFA to the European Court of Justice in Luxembourg. The court ruled that clubs could not charge a transfer fee for players whose contracts had expired. Overnight, clubs had to sign their players to longer, more lucrative contracts or risk losing their prize assets for nothing if they decided to "do a Bosman" at the end of their current deal.

Agents could make big money negotiating the bigger contracts or touting their players around for large signing-on fees.

So everyone was happy. Apart from the clubs, the game and the fans. But congratulations to the agents. You can still hear the clink of their champagne glasses now.

Not since 1966 had the nation been quite so behind the England team. As the hosts for Euro 96, there was a barely contained optimism (actually, forget the barely, the optimism was *rampant*) that football really was coming home and England would win the tournament. Skinner and Baddiel's "Three Lions" song became the unofficial national anthem and football fever gripped the country. Was it blind faith? Well, as the song says: "30 years of hurt never stopped us dreaming…"

The biggest crowd of the tournament, 76,864, squeezed in between the ever so slightly tatty twin towers of Wembley to watch the England v Scotland match. England were leading 1–0 with 13 minutes remaining when the Scots got a penalty. As McAllister ran up to take it, the ball appeared to bobble on the spot and Seaman saved. Surprisingly, the normally publicity-shy Uri Geller claimed credit for the shifting ball.

"Three Lions" fever reached, er, fever pitch with England's stunning (and almost surreal) 4–1 destruction of Holland. At one point the England players were, literally, queuing up to score against the Dutch. Hey, we really are going to win this tournament!

Oh bugger. Our chances of winning the tournament decrease somewhat after Germany beat us on penalties in the semi-final. They go on to take the trophy. Still, Gareth Southgate's penalty miss does at least earn him a lucrative gig starring in a pizza advert.

David who...?
Beckham makes his name with a goal from his own half

The 1996/97 goal of the season competition was hardly what you would call suspenseful. (Unless you were very stupid.) Because everyone knew who was going to win it when the season was only one day old. Some bloke called David Beckham...

The young Becks made the first of what would be a lifetime of headlines with an outrageous lob from just inside his own half in injury time of the

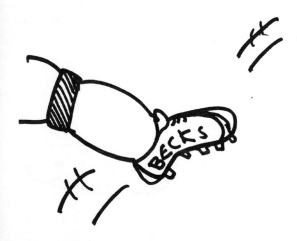

tch between Manchester United and Wimbledon. United were already
) up when Beckham decided to try his luck, leaning back and belting
ball some 57 yards. A back-tracking Neil Sullivan could only
lornly leap too late as the ball hit the back of his net. The next day's
ers had their headlines and the tabloids had a new plaything. It was
beginning of a beautiful (if occasionally turbulent) relationship.

He's an old hand...
Shilton makes his 1,000th appearance

You don't have to be mad to be a goalkeeper but... um, it is okay to be quite old. Peter Shilton made his first appearance in a green jersey (they all wore green back then, don't you know?) in 1966. Some 30 years later he stepped out at Brisbane Road for Third Division Leyton Orient to rack up his 1,000th League game and bag himself a place in the *Guinness Book of Records*.

The 47-year-old's career had taken in over half a dozen clubs and 125 appearances for England but the old geezer still managed to keep a clean sheet in match number 1,000. Mostly by waving a stick at opposing strikers and telling them to keep out of his allotment. Sorry, penalty area.

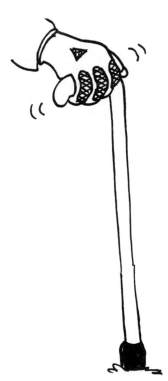

Who hates David Beckham? Er, everyone if you believed the national press. In a particularly spectacular version of their regular build 'em up and knock 'em down game, the papers went to town on the boy David after he got himself sent off in England's crucial second-round match with Argentina in the 1998 World Cup.

A petulant, but harmless, kick at Simeone drew a red card (and some very impressive theatrics from the Argentinian). The dramatic match, which also saw a great goal by Owen and a penalty shoot-out at the end, ended with England's exit from the tournament. An effigy of Beckham was hung in East London and his face became the bullseye in a tabloid newspaper's dartboard illustration. Manager Hoddle's "defence" of his midfielder ("I'm not denying he cost us the game") didn't help and Becks became Public Enemy Number One... for a while. Another tournament "highlight" included the Romanian team bleaching their hair blond in a rather bizarre show of team spirit. There was also Blanc kissing Barthez's bald bonce every game (ye-uck!) and Brazilian Ronaldo's name disappearing and reappearing on the team sheet for the final – which hosts France won.

Twist and shout

Ryan Giggs celebrates scoring the best FA Cup goal ever

'He gives defenders twisted blood," remarked Alex Ferguson once about Ryan Giggs' ability to turn opposition players inside out. After the 1999 FA Cup semi-final replay, there were more than a few Arsenal players who would have agreed (if they hadn't, of course, been busy receiving blood transfusions at the time…).

In a match packed with drama (Beckham's magnificent opener, Bergkamp's equalizer, Keane's sending-off, Schmeichel's penalty save) and steeped in significance (both Arsenal and United could still achieve a League and Cup double), there was little to separate the two best teams in the country.

Until Giggs collected a stray Arsenal pass in his own half, and proceeded to run the length of the pitch, dribble round the entire Arsenal defence (twice) and slam the ball into the roof of the net.

Impressively, he still had the energy to celebrate the winner by taking his shirt off and waving it around his head, in the process displaying one of the hairiest chests in football history.

Heart of glass
On-loan keeper saves Carlisle

There's leaving it late and then there's leaving it late. Carlisle, it can safely be said, left it late. Their 71-year stay in the Football League was, approximately, five seconds from coming to an end and they still needed to score one more goal to stave off Conference football. Cue on-loan keeper Jimmy Glass. Up for the final corner of the match he collected a clearance and thumped it into the net. Carlisle were safe.

Asked if this meant he would stay at the club, Glass rather smartly replied: "Who knows? Anything can happen in football – let's face it, I just got the winner!"

Make mine a treble
Manchester United win the lot

They called it the impossible treble but, in 1999, Manchester United were making the impossible seem, well, possible. They beat Arsenal in an FA Cup semi-final replay with 10 men and a miracle Ryan Giggs goal; they came back in Turin from 2–0 down to win 3–2 against Juventus in the Champions League; they won the title race on the last day of the season with a makeshift defence; and won the FA Cup after losing their skipper Roy Keane through injury. Now all they had to do was win the European Cup... naturally, they did it the hard way.

Without Paul Scholes and Keane, and with Giggs playing out of position, it was a lacklustre United performance in the Nou Camp against Bayern Munich. The Germans took the lead after just five minutes and some 85 minutes later, with United looking incapable of even creating a chance, the officials had already tied Bayern's colours to the trophy.

The game went into stoppage time and now, a comeback looked completely impossible. So, United, of course came back. Three minutes and two corners later United were European champions in the most dramatic fashion imaginable.

Fortunately, there was just time to tie on the correct ribbons.

Reds dance upon the Rio sands
United swap FA Cup romance for Copacabana sun

The 1999 Treble winners Manchester United's chances of immediately repeating their Treble success in 2000 were dashed somewhat when they didn't enter one of the three competitions.

To ensure England's bid to stage the 2006 World Cup would be successful, the Premiership champions were persuaded to play in the FIFA Club World Championship. FIFA chiefs cleverly scheduled the exciting new tournament right in the middle of the English season thus ensuring United would not be able to play in the passé 128-year-old FA Cup going on back at home.

It was a brilliant idea, a tournament in Rio (with easy access to the Copacabana beach) that brought together all the great clubs in the world from Raja Casablanca to Al-Nassr and, yes, even South Melbourne!

The 2,000 fans who crammed into the 73,000-capacity Maracana Stadium for United's first match against Mexican giants Necaxa clearly agreed it was the birth of a football revolution. What (an) atmosphere.

United's cold-weather training quickly paid off as they drew one, lost one and won only one of their group matches to ensure immediate elimination and maximum beach time.

The FIFA Club World Championship wasn't repeated, England didn't win the 2006 World Cup bid and Manchester United players hardly won a game of head tennis on Copacabana beach. It was a sunny new dawn for football.

MANCHESTER UNITED

Roy of the Wanderers

Hastily acquired striker proves the hero

Ah, the romance of the Cup. Ignore what you just read on the left. In 2001, Wycombe Wanderers proved that the modern game hasn't yet lost *all* its charms as they reached the semi-finals of the competition. The hero of the hour was Roy Essandoh, an until-then very unfamous striker who, rumour has it, was bought off the internet when all Wycombe's first team forwards got injured.

He struck the crucial quarter-final winner against Leicester that earned the Wanderers a place in the last four against Liverpool and reminded everyone just why the FA Cup remains a jewel in the sporting crown. (The club later denied they'd bought Roy off the internet – they said they found him on teletext. Ah well, that's all right then…)

Swede thrown into hotpot

Uproar as Sven becomes England's first foreign manager

On 7 October 2000, England lost their first World Cup 2002 qualifying match (and the final game ever to be played at Wembley). To Germany! More importantly though, the man they once called "Super Kev" (and "Mighty Mouse" and "Bubble Head") resigned as England manager claiming his tactics weren't super enough to do the job.

It was time for a change, and the FA made a decision that would drop a bespectacled Swede in the stewing pot of English football. Yes, they appointed Sven-Göran Eriksson – a FOREIGNER!

Media pundits and football legends were united in horror. Former England defender (and Republic of Ireland manager) Jack Charlton

captured the prevailing mood describing the FA's decision as "a terrible mistake".

Indeed, why give the job to an inexperienced foreigner who'd only won the Italian league, European Cup Winners Cup and Super Cup with Lazio, three Portuguese league titles with Benfica, and a Swedish championship and a Uefa Cup with IFK Gothenburg (among other trophies)? What about Alan Curbishley, John Gregory and, er, Barry Fry? The rookie Swede was surely set to join former England boss Graham "Turnip" Taylor in the tabloids' vegetable patch.

Only six flukey World Cup qualifying wins in a row postponed Sven's date with composting destiny.

5-1!
England thump Germany in World Cup qualifier

Alois Alzheimer, Nadja Auermann, Andreas Baader, Johann Sebastian Bach, Boris Becker, Ludwig van Beethoven, "Bix" Beiderbecke, Karl Benz, Otto von Bismarck, Bertolt Brecht, Gottfried Daimler, Adi Dassler, Marlene Dietrich, Albert Einstein, Gabriel Daniel Fahrenheit, H.R. Giger, Steffi Graf, Günter Grass, Franz Joseph Haydn, Heinrich Rudolf Hertz, Henry A. Kissinger, Helmut Kohl, Karl Lagerfeld, Hedy Lamarr, Karl Marx, George Simon Ohm, Wolfgang Petersen, Erwin Rommel, Claudia Schiffer, Albert Schweitzer, Wim Wenders, Ferdinand von Zeppelin, Hans Zimmer… your boys took one hell of a beating!

Once in every generation, there comes a man who raises the bar in his chosen field. In the field of football commentary that bar-raiser was Big Ron Bo Jangles Atkinson (well, until *those* comments wrecked his career).

Big Ron's verbal dexterity was wasted as a manager/sunbather, and it was only when he grabbed the microphone alongside Clive Tyldesley that his gift was revealed to the wider world and beyond. To choose just one Ron-ism would be churlish. The concise analogies (on Paul Scholes: "The boy's a bubble"), the factual insights ("They are playing above ground"), the controversial claims ("Zero-zero is a big score"), the appreciation of time and space ("He had acres of time there") and the rhetorical questions ("How are they defensively, attacking-wise?")... all these qualities combined to make Big Ron indisputably "The Ron" of modern football commentators.

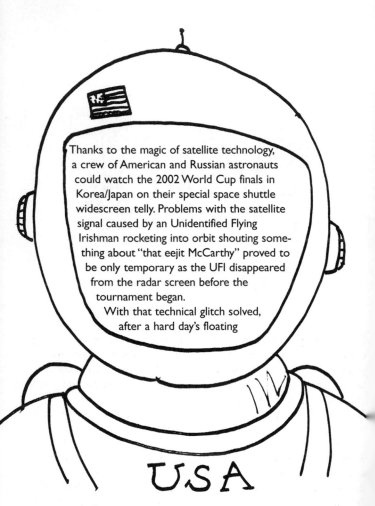

Thanks to the magic of satellite technology, a crew of American and Russian astronauts could watch the 2002 World Cup finals in Korea/Japan on their special space shuttle widescreen telly. Problems with the satellite signal caused by an Unidentified Flying Irishman rocketing into orbit shouting something about "that eejit McCarthy" proved to be only temporary as the UFI disappeared from the radar screen before the tournament began.

With that technical glitch solved, after a hard day's floating

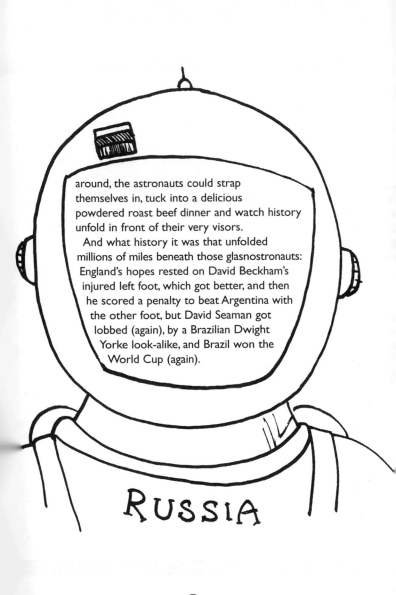

around, the astronauts could strap
themselves in, tuck into a delicious
powdered roast beef dinner and watch history
unfold in front of their very visors.

And what history it was that unfolded
millions of miles beneath those glasnostronauts:
England's hopes rested on David Beckham's
injured left foot, which got better, and then
he scored a penalty to beat Argentina with
the other foot, but David Seaman got
lobbed (again), by a Brazilian Dwight
Yorke look-alike, and Brazil won the
World Cup (again).

RUSSIA

4 Thursday

We're staying in a place called Skippy or summat like that. It's a city in a country that used to be in Yugoslavia but has moved to Macedonia. The hotel is all right, but room service ain't great. I rung down for a couple of meat pies, sausages and chips for me tea, just like me mam makes, but the bloke who took my order didn't hear me right. He sounded a bit Swedish. They sent up a fookin' chicken salad instead. I'm starvin'.

5 Friday

We did shooting practice in training today and had a good laugh. Emile's a real joker. He was hitting shots out of the ground again and again. Still hungry. I rang me agent to ask if he could fly in some food from Kenny Po's chinese in Croxteth. Could murder some sweet and sour pork balls. A lo of the boys have got these multi-coloured watches and I'm thinking of buying one. They are like Swatch watches but cost ten grand (or 35K if you want diamonds in it like Becks). Brilliant.

On 6 September 2003, manchild boy wonder Wayne Rooney became the youngest player ever to score for England at 17 years and 318 days old, beating the now old Michael Owen's previous record

6 Saturday

Rang Colleen in the morning. She wished me luck for the match against Maccy D. I love her so much, I've got a tattoo with her name on it on me arm. Jamesy told me it was illegal, cos you are not allowed to tattoo a miner. I think he was joking cos I'm a footballer, not a friggin' miner.

In the match, we woz crap in the first half and went 1–0 down. Emile came on for Lamps at half-time and all the shooting practice paid off for him when he headed it to me and I scored the equalizer. Then Becks made it 2–1 so we won. Wicked!

7 Sunday

Back in England. In the papers it says that people are starting a Monster Raving Rooney Party. Not sure I want to be a politician yet though – I'm just concentrating on me football. One of me mates rang up and invited me out for a Sunday roast, but we've got another match against Lickingties on Wednesday so I'll stick with the squad. Also, I've got to plan my 18th birthday party. Me pal Robbie says he will sing a few of his karaoke songs if I give him a signed shirt. Cheeky bugger.

Ab Fab
Roman Abramovich turns Chelsea into Chelski

Money can't buy you love (well maybe monkey love) but it can buy you a football team. And success. Probably. Or at least that's what Roman Abramovich was hoping he'd get for the several billion pounds (roughly) that he decided to invest in Chelsea to convert them into Chelski (and champions).

The Russian billionaire initially hoped to achieve footballing alchemy by combining vast sums of cash, Claudio Ranieri's strange tactical decisions and, er, John Terry. As history has shown, and another of our astonishing exclusives exclusively reveals (see screengrab of Roman's alleged desktop, circa 2003, below) that was just the beginning of his plans…

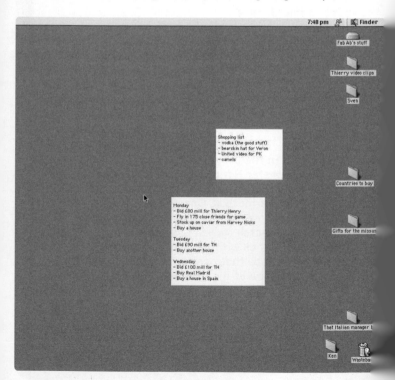

Pizzagate!
Sir Alex gets splatted in the "Battle of the Buffet"

Forget "Watergate", "Nipplegate" (was it really a "wardrobe malfunction", Ms. Jackson?) or South Park's "Closetgate" (too libellous to even comment on…), we want an answer to the most important "gate" question of all: who threw the pizza that hit Fergie?

The Manchester United boss's mug got an extra topping of tomato puree and cheese during the infamous "Battle of the Buffet" at Old Trafford in October 2004. United had just beaten Arsenal 2–0, to end the Gunners' 49-game unbeaten Premiership sequence. It had been an ill-tempered match, but sparks (and food) really flew afterwards when players and staff scuffled in the tunnel, as eye-witness and literary giant Ashley Cole would later relate in his autobiography: "This slice of pizza came flying over my head and hit Fergie straight in the mush … all mouths gawped to see this pizza slip off this famous, puce face and roll down his nice black suit."

Evocative stuff, indeed, and raising the delicious possibility that the slice was actually aimed at Cole and thrown by a United player. No wonder no-one's owned up…

103 The Miracle of Istanbul

Resurrected Liverpool shock Milan and clinch fifth European Cup

Whether it's some plumber from Droitwich claiming the face of Jesus Christ appeared to him on a prawn cocktail crisp or Nick Clegg insisting the Lib Dems will actually keep an election manifesto promise, nowadays it is hard to believe in miracles. But Liverpool supporters who experienced the 2005 UEFA Champions League final on 25 May 2005, tend to be less cynical.

Four-times European Cup winners Liverpool went into the match at the Atatürk Olympic Stadium, Istanbul, as favourites to lose to six-times champions AC Milan. Three-nil down at half-time to goals from Paolo Maldini and Hernan Crespo (two), the outlook was grim indeed for Rafa Benitez's side, but they produced a stunning second-half comeback, scoring three goals (Steven Gerrard, Vladimir Smicer and Xabi Alonso) in six minutes to level the scores.

Some sterling Liverpool defending and goalkeeping heroics from Jerzy Dudek ensured that the score stayed at 3–3 till the end of extra time. And when the outstretched left hand of Dudek palmed away Andrei Shevchenko's effort in the penalty shoot-out, the European Cup was theirs. Proper miraculous, it was.

Come on you WAGs!

While the "Golden Generation" fail to deliver the goods at the 2006 World Cup, their WAGs buy them...

The 2006 World Cup staged in Germany was supposed to be the tournament when England's so-called "Golden Generation" came of age and finally emulated the boys of '66. There was JT and Rio at the back, Stevie G and Lamps bossing the midfield and "our Wayne" up front. And with "Goldenballs" himself, Becks, wearing the captain's armband while legendary contract negotiator/ladies man Sven stood emotionless on the touchline, what could possibly go wrong? But after wins against mighty Paraguay, Trinidad & Tobago and Ecuador (not forgetting a glorious 2–2 draw with Sweden), it did. In the quarter-finals against Portugal, Rooney got himself sent off (with a little help from winking winger Cristiano Ronaldo, his loyal Manchester United team-mate) and England lost 3–1 on penalties after a thrilling goalless 120 minutes.

Never mind, at least the England players' wives and girlfriends enjoyed themselves. The WAGs did their bit for the local economy, emerging from the £1,000-a-night Brenner's Park hotel to hit the boutiques of the sleepy spa town of Baden-Baden and splash a reported £57,000 on clothes and shoes in an hour.

On the weekend, Frank Lampard's then girlfriend Elen Rives was pictured in Maxi's, the local nightclub, dancing on the table and singing along to "I Will Survive". Sadly, the same couldn't be said for Sven.

105 ZZ blows his top
Zidane turns billy goat in swansong match

Zinedine Zidane. Winner of Serie A (twice), the Italian Cup, UEFA Super Cup, Intercontinental Cup with Juventus … deep breath … and La Liga, Spanish Super Cup (twice), UEFA Champions League, UEFA Super Cup, Intercontinental Cup with Real Madrid … oh yes, and he was named European Footballer of the Year once, FIFA World Player of the Year three times and best European Player of the Past 50 Years in 2004… among other honours.

But what will the French skillster really be remembered for? For felling Italian defender Marco Materazzi with a sweet chest-nut during the 2006 World Cup final of course!

"Zizou" was looking to lift the World Cup for a second time in his last match before retirement. And it was all going swimmingly when he put France ahead with a penalty kick after seven minutes, but with the score 1–1 in extra time, Materazzi tugged at the great man's shirt.

"If you want my shirt that badly, I'll give it to you at the end of the match," offered ZZ. "I'd prefer your *puttana* of a sister," replied Marco tactfully.

Apparently, *puttana* is not a very nice thing to call someone, so Zidane promptly nutted his tormentor and got sent off. France ended up losing on penalties, but French fans soon forgave their brooding superstar's faux pas – within weeks, a subtle little ditty called *Coupe de Boule* (that's "headbutt" in French, folks) topped the Gallic pop charts.

English football journalists were in mourning following the departure of Jose Mourinho from Chelsea in September 2007. Since Mourinho strolled into Stamford Bridge and declared himself "a special one", then backed up his boast by leading Chelsea to their first league title for half a century, his penchant for bold statements had hacks hanging on his every word.

Mourinho usually had some sort of conspiracy theory to explain Chelsea's rare defeats. Or even a goalless draw, like the 2005 Carling Cup semi-final first leg with Manchester United when he claimed Sir Alex Ferguson had influenced the referee ("I know the referee did not walk to the dressing rooms alone at half time"). And he once seemed to compare Arsène Wenger to a peeping tom for commenting on Chelsea affairs ("It is a sickness") ... which was a bit out of order.

Post-Chelsea, Mourinho led Internazionale to the first "Treble" in Italian history before taking up the reins at Real Madrid. Chelsea haven't fared so well. Asked why, Jose shrugged: "It's no coincidence that their decline happened after I left." Annoyingly, it's true.

"Oh Special One, why did you have to leave us so soon?"

On 1 August 2006, following defeats in three successive major tournament quarter-finals under Sven-Göran Eriksson (and failing to persuade Luis Felipe Scolari to replace him), the FA appointed an Englishman, Stephen "Steve" McClaren, to reawaken the spirit of St George.

A radical thinker, one of McClaren's first decisions was to drop national treasure David Beckham from the squad saying he was taking "a different direction". By May 2007, and with England's Euro 2008 qualifying campaign hitting the skids, he changed direction back again and recalled Becks to the squad.

That November, under cover of an official FA umbrella-ella-ella, McClaren glumly watched England lose their final group match, 3–2 to Croatia at Wembley, thus missing out on the European Championship finals for the first time in 24 years. The next day, "The wally with the brolly" was fired after just 18 games in 16 months making his tenure the shortest-ever of any England manager.

And the FA decided that it was probably better to get a foreigner as manager after all. Enter Italian Bo' Selecta Mel B lookalike, Fabio Capello.

The 132 million dollar man!

Real Madrid break the bank for Ronaldo

There was only one Ronaldo. Remember him? The Brazilian striker, three-times FIFA World Player of the Year, who liked his food. And then there was another one – preening, six-packing, dribbling, goalscoring, moisturizing, perma-Ronsealed Portuguese football genius, Cristiano Ronaldo dos Santos Aveiro, who could turn out to be even better.

Real Madrid certainly thought so, shelling out a world-record fee of £80 million (that's €94 million or $132 million) to bring him from Manchester United to join their Galácticos in the summer of 2009, smashing (as Richard Keys would say) the previous highest mark, a measly £56 million Real had paid AC Milan for Kaka just a few weeks earlier.

Ronaldo's six-year contract was said to be worth £11 million per year, making him the highest-paid player in the world too. And that'll buy you a lot of pairs of tight-fitting swimming shorts.

Beach-slapping for Liverpool
Bent shot deflects off inflatable to deflate Reds

When Liverpool Football Club's merchandizing department launched an official club beach set, consisting of a small duffel bag, towel and inflatable ball, all for a tenner, little did they realize it would contribute to one of the most bizarre goals ever.

In the opening minutes of a game at the Stadium of Light in October 2009, a young Reds fan, obviously trying to evoke the spirit of summer on an autumnal day, punched the beach ball onto the pitch. And it was red faces all round as Sunderland striker Darren Bent fired a shot (with the real ball) which goalkeeper Pepe Reina appeared to have covered until it ricocheted off the bobbling inflatable and into the net.

According to the rulebook, the stray ball should have been considered an outside agent and play restarted with a drop-ball. Referee Mike Jones didn't seem to know that though, allowed the goal to stand and the Black Cats ran out 1–0 winners. Unsurprisingly, victorious Sunderland manager Steve Bruce backed Jones, saying: "If anyone knew that rule, then you are one saddo."

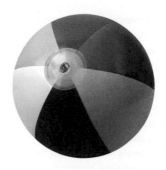

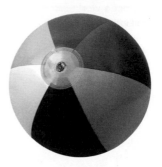

Tevez socks it to Neville
Carlos adds new term to the football lexicon

Gary Neville has never been short of an opinion, especially when it comes to rivals of his beloved Manchester United. But he picked on the wrong man, when he spoke about former team-mate Carlos Tevez's transfer to Manchester City before the 2010 Carling Cup semi-final clash between the local rivals. Neville claimed the Argentinian was "not worth" the £25 million City paid for him, backing up a previous statement by United manager Sir Alex Ferguson.

When Tevez scored a penalty in City's 2–1 first-leg win at Eastlands, he ran over to remonstrate with his tormentor who was warming up on the touchline at the time. "Shut your trap, keep quiet," he told Neville, eliciting an curt, one-fingered salute in response.

Speaking in his native language in a radio interview on ESPN Argentina later, Tevez's rage had hardly cooled: "He acted like a complete sock-sucker when he said I wasn't worth £25 million, just to suck up to the manager, I don't know what the hell that idiot is talking about me for."

Whatever the rights and wrongs of the spat, schoolchildren around Britain now had a new term to describe fellow pupils toadying up to teacher. *Muchas gracias*, Carlos.

111 Horny issue
Vuvuzelas bring a buzz to the 2010 World Cup

Millions of people around the world settled down to watch the opening game of the 2010 World Cup between South Africa and Mexico on telly. Within minutes, millions of those millions were grasping for the mute button screaming "What the **** is that noise?" Turns out the unrelenting, monotone, swarm-of-angry-bees-in-a-blender sound was being emitted by three-foot-long plastic horns known as vuvuzelas.

The vuvuzela, first used by South Africa fans to support their team, can pump out sound up to 10 decibels above the human pain threshold causing permanent hearing loss. Players complained they couldn't hear their team-mates for the din and TV broadcasters (unsuccessfully) sought technical ways to dampen the sound. FIFA supremo Sepp Blatter resisted calls to ban the horn, though, saying it would be wrong to "Europeanize" the tournament. Quite right too, although cycling legend/football fan/Twitter enthusiast Lance Armstrong spoke for many when he tweeted: "No offence to the vuvuzela posse but, man, it's a bit much."

The woe of England's No.6

Goalkeeping howler tickles worldwide web jokers

Poor old Robert Green. The self-deprecating West Ham goalkeeper, who wore gloves bearing the legend, "England's No. 6", following his omission from Fabio Capello's first-ever England squad, later impressed so much that he was the Italian's choice to stand between the sticks in England's first match of the World Cup 2010 against the United States.

Green let the chance slip through his fingers though. Literally. With England coasting at 1–0, Green allowed a pea-rolling Clint Dempsey shot to beat him and trickle into the net, costing England two points and ensuring

that he would watch the remainder of the tournament from the bench.

Over the following days, Green would need his sense of humour as the inevitable jokes did the rounds on the internet. Far be it from us to remind him of them all again now… Okay, just a couple:

"Steven Gerrard said: 'The whole team is behind Robert Green'. With hindsight, that's a good place to stand."

"My computer's got the Robert Green virus. It can't save anything."

And in conclusion…

"Kermit was right. It's not easy being Green."

113 Across the line
Echoes of '66, Hursty, the Russian linesman and all
that as the Germans finally get goal-line payback

By the time England played Germany in the 2010 World Cup quarter-final at the Free State Stadium in Bloemfontein, South Africa, it had been 44 years of hurt since the Three Lions stood proudly atop the world of football. But the gleam of Jules Rimet faded further as a spritely young German team crushed Fabio Capello's underperformers, 4–1.

However, England definitely would have won if it hadn't been for a dodgy goal-line decision (and if you ignore England's diabolical defending and the Germans' dominance for 90 per cent of the game).

With Germany leading 2–1 after 38 minutes, Frank Lampard's chipped shot hit the underside of the crossbar. The ball clearly bounced down over the line but, to general bewilderment, the referee waved play on. It was a bit like '66 all over again, only different.

Instant replays highlighted the glaring error, but none of the five officials on the pitch were actually allowed to use video evidence to see what a ricket they'd made of it.

Afterwards, Capello claimed "that one goal would have made the game completely different". Captain Stevie G admitted that to say "that's the reason we got beat would be a lie". Meanwhile, Lamps said the introduction of goal-line technology was a "no brainer".

But would the FIFA brains trust agree and cross the line into the brave new world of video evidence? Er, no.

Diego returns to WC action!

Maradona makes his mark as World Cup coach

When the Argentine Football Federation appointed maverick national icon Diego Maradona as their head coach to lead them to the 2010 World Cup finals, it was probably with the same trepidation that Charlie Sheen's PR people feel when they let him off the leash to do a TV interview.

And Diego didn't disappoint in qualification, deploying an incredible total of 108 players over 18 months, playing a series of bonkers formations and getting banned by FIFA for two months for a foul-mouthed rant against critics following the 1–0 win over Uruguay which secured Argentina's place at the finals.

Maradona then left out two stars of Internazionale's Treble-winning team – Esteban Cambiasso and Mario Zanetti – from his finals squad, but included defender Ariel Garcé who'd helped mighty Colón to 14th place in the Argentinian League. Rumours that this was because Garcé was the only face Diego could recall from a dream he'd had of his team winning the World Cup remain unconfirmed.

A luxury toilet, featuring heated seat, front and rear bidet wands and a warm air blow dryer, was installed in Diego's room at Argentina's base camp in South Africa after his aides claimed exisiting facilities did not meet his high standards. Come the tournament proper, Diego ordered the losing team in training games to bend over and have balls fired at their backsides, and dispensed hugs and kisses to Lionel Messi and co. with gay abandon. For a while the touchy-feely approach seemed to work for his boys, until the Germans drilled them 4–0 in the quarter-finals and Diego's dream went down the toilet.

Football was the winner at the 2010 World Cup. Well, Spain actually won the tournament, adding to their Euro 2008 success, and they did so with a thrilling style of football specifically designed for diddy men.

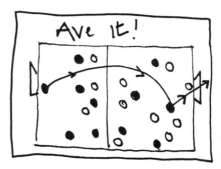

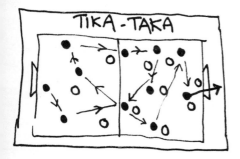

Known as "tiki-taka" (that's the Spanish name for the juggling toy, clackers), Spanish commentator Andrés Montes is usually credited with first applying the term to Spain's artful short-pass-and-move tactics.

Playing to the strengths of their technically skilled but slightly built midfield playmakers, Andrés Iniesta and Xavi (a pair so good they often consigned Arsenal superstar and fellow tiki-taka disciple Cesc Fabregas to the bench), Spain left opponents dizzy with Pollockesque patterns of possession. Many pundits said tiki-taka was even better to watch than Holland's "Total Football" of 1974. Others claimed it was even more exciting than Subbuteo. Only with smaller players. Tiki-taka-tastic!

England win bid to host World Cup 2018...

... Oh no, they don't!

After losing out to Germany in their bid to stage the 2006 World Cup, England 2018 Chief Executive Andy Anson called for a dose of humility this time, saying they "Must not fall victim to arrogance". It's not clear that the English tabloid press got the memo in the build-up to decision day though, and the vibe was less humble, more "It's coming home, it's coming home. Football's coming home… "

All the big guns were wheeled out for the results ceremony, including the omnipresent Becks, HRH Prince William and bum-faced Prime Minister David Cameron. But when the FIFA supremo Sepp Blatter opened the envelope, Russia had won. Turns out England got just two votes from FIFA's 22 delegates.

The *Sun* responded with the sober headline, "And the 2018 World Cup is awarded to… mafia state". Blatter accused the English of, um, "arrogance", saying he couldn't believe the reaction of "England, the motherland of fair play ideas." And in fairness, Russia have never hosted a World Cup before, whereas England have. Then again, as Tony Adams once said, "If life was fair, it would be called 'fair', but it's not, it's called 'life'", so we'll complain anyway.

117 The Dali of the Premier League

Analogy-spouting Blackpool boss Ian Holloway
hits the big stage

When Blackpool were promoted to England's top flight in 2010 for
the first time since 1971, the Premier League instantly became a more
colourful (well, tangerineful, to be precise) place. And while the sea
of orange shirts lit up the stands like, er, the Blackpool Illuminations,
Seasiders' manager Ian Holloway delighted pressmen by evoking
Dali-esque imagery (sort of) to describe the joys and tribulations
of club football at the highest level.

Holloway has a long history of
"giving good quote", once
describing a run of bad luck
thus: "Right now, everything is
going wrong for me – if I fell
in a barrel of boobs, I'd come
out sucking my thumb."

Blackpool FC always
looked like a good match
for Holloway too – as the
man himself once said: "I
like Blackpool. We're very
similar. We both look
better in the dark."

He soon suggested video technology operated by a chimpanzee ("with not much training") and compared a scrappy win to larceny ("If you're a burglar, it's no good poncing about outside somebody's house, looking good with your swag bag ready. Just get in there, burgle them and come out. I don't advocate that obviously, it's just an analogy.").

Holloway maintained his form in the Premier League, likening Stoke's use of long-throw tactics to a cake ingredient ("Call that cinammon"), pimpin' old football clichés ("There was a spell in the second half when I took my heart off my sleeve and put in my mouth") and enlivening even the most mundane enquiries…
"Ian, have you got any injury worries?"
"No, I'm fully fit, thank you."

In January 2011, two stalwarts of Sky Sports' football coverage, Andy Gray and Richard Keys, were, respectively, sacked and forced to resign when their sexist off-air comments were leaked. Yes, we know, the idea that sexist attitudes could still exist in the enlightened world of football is unbelievable. Next they'll be telling us that some footballers are gay!

The storm broke when Keys and Gray were caught ridiculing female assistant referee Sian Massey before a game between Liverpool and Wolves. Among other gems, Gray confided: "Women don't understand the offside law."

"'Course they don't," replied his sidekick.

Sky researchers, obviously desperate to help the star presenters, soon leaked more off-air footage of Gray making lewd comments and gestures to a female colleague, while Keys was seen asking Jamie Redknapp, "Did you smash it?" (and he wasn't talking about a 30-yard free-kick).

Keys issued a *mea culpa* on talkSPORT radio, during which he apologized for the "prehistoric banter", but his resignation was inevitable and the two dinosaurs' fate was sealed. Yep, they got a show on talkSPORT.

"Sexist? Us? Do me a favour love... and put the kettle on"

Olympic tenancy tussle
West Ham and Spurs both go for the vacancy at the
Olympic Stadium... and the Hammers get the nod

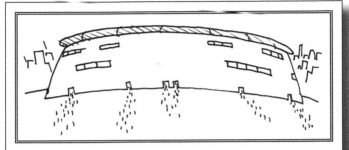

TO LET
STADIUM, STRATFORD E15

- Fabulous £537 million, state-of-the-art stadium, scheduled for
  completion in 2011
- Available for rent after minor sporting event in summer 2012
- 80,000 seats (including 55,000 temporary ones, for some reason, so
  will need another £100 million-ish spent on it)
- Athletics track and grass pitch suitable for football, cricket, rugby
  league, local community tug-of-war events... and athletics
- Fabric membrane roof that looks like an upside-down paper hat
- Toilet facilities built from recycled shipping containers
- Massive 115-metre curly-wurly steel statue. Bigger than the Statue
  of Liberty!
- Brand-new, high-speed transport links to central London which cost
  a few quid
- Attractive property for North London clubs who don't mind
  abandoning their fans and tradition to move to the East End, killing
  the existing local community club, Leyton Orient (it's all about the
  legacy, folks), and keeping the athletics track which we guarantee will
  destroy match atmosphere

For full-colour brochure, please contact b.johnson @ borisbikes.co.uk

They think it's all over...

... It is now for owl mascot

And so we reach the final "minute" of extra-time in our concise (and, admittedly, somewhat schizoid) summary of football history. And, lordy, hasn't the game come a long way since those olde pancake-tossers were chasing a ball through the village and kicking each other up the arse? Which is fair enough, as that was 900 years ago.

Come 2011, there were oil-rich sheikhs trying to make Roman Abramovich look tight-fisted by shovelling cash into Manchester City and Abramovich proving he's not by paying Liverpool £50 million for Jose Torres. All the while FIFA bigwigs were fretting about whether wearing snoods could endanger players necks. A different world.

But occasionally we get reminders of the anarchic roots of the game, such as during a Colombian first division game between Junior de Barranquilla and Deportivo Pereira in February 2011, when the home team's mascot, an owl (a real one), was accidentally hit by a ball and then deliberately punted off the pitch by callous Deportivo defender Luis Moreno. Amid death threats and general global outrage, Moreno later claimed, "It wasn't my intention to hurt the animal." By kicking it? Hmm.

Sadly, the owl later passed away, but football, like Celine Dion's heart, will go on.